TRUST AND OBEY

TRUST AND OBEY

Explorations in
Evangelical Spirituality

DAVID K. GILLETT

DARTON·LONGMAN+TODD

First published in 1993 by
Darton, Longman and Todd Ltd
1 Spencer Court
140–142 Wandsworth High Street
London SW18 4JJ

ISBN 0-232-51899-8

A catalogue record for this book is available
from the British Library

Unless otherwise stated
the quotations from the Bible are taken from
the New Revised Standard Version

Phototypeset by Intype, London
Printed and bound in Great Britain
at the University Press, Cambridge

CONTENTS

PREFACE

To attempt a systematic exposition of evangelical spirituality is to look at evangelicalism in a way that it has not normally thought of itself. The general evangelical approach to faith is prescriptive, rather than descriptive; we like to say, 'This is the gospel – this is biblical truth.' The task of spirituality is more descriptive. In this book I have tried as much as possible to be descriptive, but as that would have been too bland on its own, I have not held back from expressing my own views on the glories and weaknesses of evangelicalism as I see it.

Inevitably much of what I have written will reflect my personal convictions – however fair I believe myself to have been! As far as possible I have sought to build up the picture from historical sources that represent mainstream evangelicalism in any particular period. Nevertheless, my own background and spiritual formation, together with the approaches beyond evangelicalism which have had an influence upon me, have inevitably coloured my perceptions to a greater or lesser extent – and at times I may be less aware of this than others. To help the reader who wishes to approach this book from a source- or tradition-critical approach, I will give some clues, by listing the main landmarks in my own spiritual journey.

Since my conversion as a sixth-former from an intellectually fashionable atheism I have been nurtured for many years within a definite evangelical tradition. I was a convinced member and president of the Christian Union while at university; after reading theology as an undergraduate I studied at an evangelical theological college. I served a curacy in a conservative evangelical parish, and then worked for a national evangelical youth movement committed to encouraging evangelism and discipleship among young people through the life of the local church.

This was followed by a spell of teaching in an evangelical theological college – different from the one I had attended. Along the way I had moved from a staunchly anti-charismatic position (I still have sermons in my filing system that gently, but definitely denounce *charismata* as spurious) to a personal commitment and involvement. Then came three years as part of an ecumenical community of Catholics and Protestants working for renewal and reconciliation in Northern Ireland. The ecumenical and charismatic input began an ongoing commitment to explore more widely than my evangelical formation had encouraged, and that has led me since into an ever-deepening study of, and sharing in, the spiritual tradition of the Church, East and West.

In that study I have been earthed by my move back to England as a vicar in a large urban parish whose tradition was a mixture of anglo-catholic, charismatic and evangelical. But more powerful than these traditions were the demands of the situation which led to a deeper discovery of the power and breadth of the gospel, faced by so many needs – emotional and social. It was the residents of Lewsey Farm in Luton who moulded the various strands of my own background and study into an integration and wholeness by the sheer force and necessity of Christian commitment: for them, faith was in no sense a bonus – it was life itself.

After that, it was back into my third evangelical theological college, this time as principal, where, hopefully, I continue my learning in company with today's students. For most, in our college community, evangelical commitment is central, but an increasing number are committed to exploring the biblical roots of faith as they are diversely expressed within the richness of the church's story.

I write with a deep sense of gratitude for, and commitment to, my evangelical heritage. I also believe strongly that one's spiritual roots must not be jettisoned, but are to be explored and encouraged to produce ever stronger growth in the present. I do this in the confident expectation that one's journey is greatly enriched by learning to appreciate the life of the Spirit of God which flows more fully in other spiritual traditions than most of us realize.

DAVID GILLETT
Trinity College, Bristol

ACKNOWLEDGEMENTS

I am grateful to D. R. Gould for permission to quote from 'May the mind of Christ my Saviour' by Katie Wilkinson (*Christian Praise* Hymn 348); to the Methodist Publishing House for permission to quote from Hymns 98, 256, 359, 360, 443 and 761 by Charles Wesley in the *Methodist Hymn Book*; and to Thankyou Music for permission to quote from 'From heaven you came' by Graham Kendrick (*Songs of Fellowship* Hymn 120) copyright © 1983 Thankyou Music, PO Box 75, Eastbourne, East Sussex BN23 6NW, UK.

1

DISCOVERING EVANGELICAL SPIRITUALITY

I recall, on one occasion, going to a retreat house to lead a session entitled 'Evangelical Spirituality' as part of a series designed to look at a broad range of spiritualities within the Church. It was clear to me that the majority of the people on the course were puzzled by the subject; most had no helpful experience of personal encounters with evangelical spirituality; others were rather apprehensive about what they thought it might be; and some were plainly surprised that there *was* such a thing!

This was due, in part no doubt, to the relative isolation of evangelicalism from many other traditions within the Church. It is also the kind of situation that has been fostered by the traditional hesitancy within evangelicalism to see itself as just *one* of many Christian spiritual traditions. This tendency within historic evangelicalism (as within certain other traditions!) has often meant that it regards itself as the true way, with a crusading zeal in relation to the rest of the Church to root out heresy and convert all to a thoroughgoing evangelicalism.

A New Openness

Spirituality is certainly a new area of study with which evangelicals have begun to grapple in the last few decades. Previously spirituality was seen as a word that describes the systems and methods of prayer of the various schools of catholic and orthodox spirituality; it was concerned with mystical and ascetical theology; it was often seen to be dealing with the realms of monasticism and withdrawal from the world in order to seek solitude and holiness; and it was thought to exhibit a strong dependence on priests and sacerdotalism. On these criteria, evangelicals did not have a spirituality, and, for the most part, *would not want one*! They have felt that they did not need a set of exercises or spiritual guides to direct them through their Christian life. That was all part of the system rejected at the Protestant Reformation in the sixteenth century. Traditionally, evangelicals 'are suspicious of scholastic and mystical spirituality and fear that the Carmel we are bidden ascend may be the Sinai of bondage, and all our asceticism dead works.'[1]

The evangelical approach to religion is that our freedom of access to God, the availability and comprehensibility of the scriptures to all, and the priesthood of all believers, render unnecessary all reliance on systems and special intermediaries to foster growth in the spiritual life. As Christianity is, in essence, a personal relationship between the individual and God, growth occurs naturally and uniquely in so far as the person remains open to the work of the Spirit of God within his or her life.

Within the last few decades, however, a sea change has occurred within evangelicalism. At least for a growing number, the barricades are down; the belief that truth resides only within the evangelical tradition is nowhere near as widespread as it once was. There remains a fundamental commitment to biblical essentials and theological orthodoxy: in matters of belief, evangelicals, almost by definition, will always want to stand for the principle that all theology should be consistent with the revealed Word of God in scripture, and that certain cardinal doctrines are non-negotiable. Because of that, many others will always find evangelicals somewhat uncomfortable and prickly bedfellows. By its very inner nature, this is almost bound to be so, as from its beginnings, evangelicalism has been a crusading, reforming and renewing movement, and, as we shall see, that characteristic remains essential to its nature. It will always manifest a certain grain-in-the-oyster-shell quality. But today there is much evidence to show that it is happier to see itself described in this

---

[1] Article on 'Spirituality' in Gordon Wakefield (ed.), *A Dictionary of Christian Spirituality* (London, SCM Press 1983), p. 362.

way, rather than as the cuckoo-in-the-nest, which is how it has sometimes appeared.

This book is written with the conviction that evangelicalism represents one of the important spiritualities, or more accurately, *groups* of spiritualities, within the Church. It is a tradition which needs to live in mutual openness with others so that there can be increasing cross-fertilization. It should be eager to learn from other traditions as it continues its own inner development. Such processes of learning ought to appeal to evangelicalism because, at heart, its aim is to enter ever more fully into the whole breadth of biblical Christianity. Yet, for all of us, this remains a goal, for it is never totally achievable within any one person's individual walk with God, or in any specific ecclesial structure. Every one of us can only live out our own inevitably limited vision of Christian discipleship. The evangelical will always be striving for a greater wholeness of biblical vision, and so we need to explore what other Christians down the ages, and in our own time, have discovered about the work of God's grace in their lives, so that we can continue to grow into a fuller appreciation of all that is ours in Christ.

Max Warren, one of the great evangelical missionary statesmen of the twentieth century, expresses what, to my mind, is a most helpful perspective on the relationship between evangelicalism and other spiritual traditions:

> Evangelical religion is . . . the whole Christian Faith held in a particular balance. There is no question of claiming a monopoly. The evangelical is no more Christian than others who, in understanding and practice, have worked out a different balance, another proportion of Faith . . . To ignore the equal validity of different understandings of the mystery of our religion, or the equal authenticity of the experiences which result from such different understandings, is a disastrous obstacle to true Christian unity. Failure frankly to thrash out the theological significance of our differences is one reason for the paralysis which today threatens the whole movement towards Christian unity. An equal threat to any discovery of true unity is to pretend that

differences do not matter, whereas the spiritual challenge is positively to enjoy them.[2]

In this dialogue between different traditions I hope that others in the Church will perceive much that they can learn from evangelical spirituality as they begin to understand its inner essence and dynamic, and that this will enrich them in their own life of faith. Consequently, one of my aims in writing this book, is that those who have not previously felt at home with evangelicalism will discover a framework to help in understanding this tradition, and glimpse some of the richness within its heritage, which is part of the common possession of the whole Church. I also hope that evangelicals themselves will be encouraged to study in more depth the whole range of their spiritual tradition, to reflect critically upon it, and to see the links between this and other, often very different, traditions which have much from which we can learn and benefit.

In our journey, which will take us into different facets throughout the history of evangelical spirituality, it will be apparent that I speak as an Englishman and as an evangelical Anglican. I am the one by birth and the other by grace, by circumstance and by conviction: I trust that non-English and non-Anglican evangelicals will not feel that I have been too unfair to them. But before progressing any further, it is necessary to define the ways in which I am using the words 'evangelical spirituality', because they will not mean to everyone what they mean to me. We turn first to . . .

Spirituality
It is, for many, a word that is surrounded with an aura of vagueness and mystery, yet increasingly it is being used by all religions, as well as non-religious traditions, to refer to the study of the inner reality of human existence in relation to the particular life-purpose to which that religion or philosophy is committed. It reminds us that all humanity is engaged on a religious quest and that we, as Christians, are seen by many as one particular tradition within the totality of world spirituality.

It might seem a long way from evangelical spirituality to begin

---

[2] Max Warren, *Crowded Canvas* (London, Hodder and Stoughton 1974), pp. 213f.

our definition in this broad terrain of the world-wide spiritual search. However, it is a right and necessary starting point in our multi-faith world, for the presence and vitality of other religions impinge on Christian spirituality in a wholly more urgent way than in previous generations.

I remember giving a lift to a university student, in the early 1970s, who told me that he had been searching for a spirituality which was deep and meaningful for *him*. He recounted how he had tried many different churches, both in his home town and in his university city. In none of them had he found the depth of reality for which he was searching. Finally, in the Buddhist Society of his university, he discovered that longed-for depth of reality. At that time, such an encounter in Britain was rare; now, the appeal of other religions is commonplace, and Christianity here, as it has long been in other parts of the world, is seen as one spirituality among many. It is in such a context that we, as Christians, both develop our own spirituality, and seek to commend it to others.

One of the most helpful definitions of spirituality is the one which was given to contributors who were asked to write articles for the twenty-five-volume *World Spirituality* series. Spirituality was defined for them as the study that 'focuses on that inner dimension of the person called by certain traditions the spirit. This spiritual core is the deepest centre of the person. It is here that the person is open to the transcendent dimension; it is here that the person experiences ultimate reality. The series explores the discovery of this core, the dynamics of its development, and its journey to the ultimate goal. It deals with prayer, spiritual direction, the various maps of the spiritual journey, and the methods of advancement in the spiritual ascent.'[3]

This quest for inner meaning is a universal phenomenon and, if we believe in the uniqueness of Christ, that in him God has revealed the goal of all human searching and the way to peace and fellowship between us and himself, then we should be happy to live in dialogue with other religious traditions. As Christians, we must honour everyone's search for God, seek to understand it better and, without fear, be able to share with them in terms

---

[3] Ewert Cousins, *Christian Spirituality: Origins to the Twelfth Century* (Volume 16 in the series *World Spirituality*, ed. Bernard McGinn and John Meyendorf, London, Routledge & Kegan Paul 1986), p. xiii.

of the questions that *they* are asking, and relate our discovery
in Christ to those searchings.

As evangelicals have usually been slower than most to seek
to understand and enter into dialogue with those of other faiths,
it is important to lay down this marker and emphasize the
legitimately broad expanse of the study of spirituality, before we
turn to the more specific area of Christian spirituality, and then
narrow our focus even more precisely on to its evangelical
tradition.

The particular distinguishing marks of Christian spirituality
are Trinitarian, and focus on the revelation of God in Christ
who is set forth as the Way, the Truth and the Life, and by
whose death and resurrection God has provided the answer to
all humanity's need and longing. Christian spirituality, therefore,
is to do with how we articulate our relationship with God in
Christ, and the particular practical ways which we find most
helpful in developing this relationship from within the whole
range of Christian tradition and experience. Consequently it is
not merely an academic discipline, though it includes that, but
an enquiry into what God has revealed in Christ about knowing
him, and what others before us have discovered as legitimate and
helpful ways of developing that relationship, with the express
intention of growing ourselves. As such it is a study that always
leads to action – action to do with growth in prayer, in listening
to God, in obedience, and in holiness.

The task of Christian spirituality, then, is to lead to the
engagement of four different horizons:

(1)   The revelation of God in Christ as witnessed in the
      scriptures.
(2)   The various spiritual traditions and emphases within the
      history of Christianity.
(3)   The cultural and community context in which we live.
(4)   The background, experience, and personality of the indi-
      vidual.

As we grow in the understanding of revelation, of ourselves, of
our particular context, and of the variety of Christian spiritualities, so we are able to develop more appropriate and effective
ways of growing in prayer and holiness.

Evangelical

In common with most studies in church history, 'Evangelicalism' refers in this book to the clearly distinguishable family of Christian traditions which emerged following the Evangelical Revival in the eighteenth century. The movement was closely identified, from the beginning, with the brothers John and Charles Wesley, and their friend George Whitefield, as well as with a growing number of clergy whose followers remained within the Church of England.

There are those who want to assert that evangelicalism is a much older movement than that – in fact, that it is the only true and genuine expression of biblical faith from the time of the New Testament onwards. But, while there are identifiable historical roots of this tradition which do indeed go right back to the New Testament, there were such major developments within the Revival of the eighteenth century that we are forced to conclude that a new movement was born. In seeking to express the biblical faith, this new movement developed particular doctrinal emphases, social attitudes, priorities in mission and forms of spirituality, and through all the developments of the last 250 years these characteristics are still reflected today in the evangelical tradition. The family likeness remains, but it is a family that now looks much more like an extended family with all its aunts, uncles and cousins, than the tightly-knit nuclear family living within the same small terraced house.

But evangelicalism is not simply all of those who are the historical descendants of the eighteenth-century revival. There are some who have so moved from the essentials of their evangelical roots that they would no longer describe themselves as evangelical. Consequently, in addition to *describing* evangelicalism as a historical movement we have to face the difficult question of *defining* the doctrinal boundaries of evangelical belief. John Stott has given us what is perhaps the shortest definition, namely that evangelicals are *Bible people* and *gospel people*.[4] In spite of its brevity, this definition manages to encapsulate the essence of evangelicalism, but everything then depends on the exposition given to these two characteristics.

---

[4] Originally given as the main point in the closing address of the National Evangelical Anglican Congress held at Nottingham in 1977.

Jim Packer[5] expands the definition to six essential features that, by their particular combination, mark out evangelicalism from other Christian traditions – the supremacy of Holy Scripture, the majesty of Jesus Christ, the Lordship of the Holy Spirit, the necessity of conversion, the priority of evangelism, and the importance of fellowship.

David Bebbington[6] takes another, more descriptive and historical approach, which is a particularly helpful framework in tracing the differences and similarities in evangelical spirituality through the changes of the last two centuries and more. He sees four characteristics that have remained constant features within this development. He calls them *Conversionism*, *Activism*, *Biblicism*, and *Crucicentrism*. Essentially these mean:

(1) The conviction that lives need to be changed by a personal encounter with Christ.
(2) A commitment to a life of energetic service for the gospel, particularly in evangelism.
(3) A concern to uphold the primacy and authority of the scriptures.
(4) A confidence in the power of the cross and its centrality both to the gospel and to Christian discipleship.

Whether we speak of evangelicalism in terms of doctrinal definition or historical description, no formula in the end will suit every evangelical, but hopefully in this book, all varieties of evangelicals will recognize the family likenesses, even if their cousins who live in another country with a different climate seem to have developed some markedly unaccustomed, and to their eyes, not very elegant, features![7]

[5] J. I. Packer, *The Evangelical Anglican Identity Problem* (Oxford, Latimer House 1978), pp. 20–23.

[6] David Bebbington, *Evangelicalism in Modern Britain* (London, Unwin Hyman 1989), pp. 5–17.

[7] Although the word 'evangelical' is used consistently through this book to refer to a particular historical and spiritual tradition within the Church, it is too important and central a word to be hijacked by one particular group. In its essential meaning, *gospel-like*, it is a word which belongs to the whole Church in which many individuals, groups and traditions are rightly described as evangelical because they embody, in a particularly distinctive way, some notable gospel characteristics but who would not fall within the boundaries of the evangelical movement.

The study of evangelical spirituality is thus a combination of research (both historical and contemporary), description, analysis, evaluation, and commitment to discovering the agenda for spiritual growth and development, both personal and corporate. This kind of study differs in several ways from the approaches which normally govern works on evangelical faith and belief. There the task is usually seen as more dogmatic, centring on explanation, definition and prescription about what is biblical and what is not. In studying the spirituality of a tradition we are seeking to go beneath theological definition to discover the life of faith and prayer which is the way in which people interpret the tradition in actual lived experience. In thus seeking to understand the living tradition of a community's spirituality, we are often looking at experiences, beliefs and attitudes which are far nearer to some in other traditions than the particular language of those traditions would suggest.

A Tradition, not a System

Evangelical spirituality is difficult to locate because it is continually evolving. This constant evolution is due in large measure to the centrality of the personal encounter with Christ which is more fundamental than commitment to particular ecclesial structures. It reflects also the desire to search the scriptures for God's truth and to re-examine the contemporary experience of Christians in the light of scripture, rather than to depend on any inherited theological system. Charles Simeon, one of the leading evangelical Church of England clergymen of the eighteenth century, used to say, 'We want Bible Christians, not system Christians.' The Church's tradition is seen as subservient to the primary authority of the Bible which, through the illumination of the Holy Spirit, is accessible to every individual believer.

There is often, of course, a much greater dependence on an unacknowledged tradition, with somewhat less biblical radicalism than is realized. In fact, once evangelicals accept as biblical truth a particular interpretation on any point, they can become strangely impervious to allowing the scriptures to challenge their thinking. Evangelicalism has frequently moved forward when some of its received biblical orthodoxy has been vigorously challenged by a rising generation.

A significant example of this challenge to supposed biblical orthodoxy in spirituality is seen in the challenge to the rather negative, somewhat taboo-ridden evangelical spirituality of the middle years of this century. In the book, *I Wish I Had Known* . . . published in 1968, one of the contributors wrote:

> The error of my thinking, like that of the Pharisees, was in the fact that the particular actions on which I evaluated myself and others were actually matters on which the Bible fails to speak clearly. The daily Quiet Time, while having many good reasons in its support, is not commanded in the Scriptures . . . The fear of association with non-Christians in their social activities, too, is not in accord with Jesus' example . . . To break out of this deeply conditioned way of thinking, I had to deny in my own behaviour the false proposition on which I had been living.[8]

In the years since then a growing openness to change has been evident within evangelicalism and, consequently, its spirituality has changed and developed into ever greater diversity. Such changes inevitably make it more difficult to locate what might be called an 'authentic version' of evangelical spirituality. This task has been rendered even more complex by the emergence of a major new emphasis which has radically affected much evangelicalism in the last quarter of the twentieth century.

The Influence of Charismatic Renewal

Many strands of evangelicalism have assimilated the emphases of charismatic spirituality as this renewal movement has penetrated historic churches as well as bringing new churches into being. While some evangelicals have sought to resist all semblance of charismatic influence, many have thoroughly assimi-

---

[8] *I wish I had known* (London, Scripture Union 1968), p. 84 in the chapter attributed to M. Svoboda, a pseudonym. All the fifteen chapters were written under pseudonyms as the climate of the times made 'breaking ranks' with what was the perceived and biblical evangelical position too risky for the writers, some of whom were well known in evangelical circles.

lated some or all of its spirituality, or at least been affected to varying degrees in their spirituality, without adopting a basic charismatic theological framework. So pervasive has been the influence of charismatic spirituality that there can be very few expressions of evangelicalism that have not been affected by its presence, even if the only effect has been in the area of defining oneself as distinct from the newer movement; very few have ignored it altogether.

Although charismatic renewal is not to be found only within evangelicalism, many of its theological and spiritual roots are the same as those of that tradition. In essence, charismatic renewal has many of the marks of an evangelical renewal movement in whatever ecclesial context it occurs. In more catholic, radical and liberal traditions it usually brings greater emphasis on the scriptures, the centrality of the person and work of Jesus in the experience of the individual believer, a confidence in the supernatural dimensions of the gospel, and a commitment to evangelism – all of which are traditionally central within evangelicalism.

Because of its particular nature, charismatic emphases have often found a fairly congenial home within an evangelicalism that is open to exploration and discovery and in the United Kingdom it has most obviously been within this section of the Church that it has taken root. (This is not to deny the significance of charismatic renewal within other traditions, especially the world-wide phenomenon of Roman Catholic charismatic renewal.) In remoulding many aspects of evangelical spirituality, charismatic renewal has been one of the most obvious factors in encouraging evangelicalism to broaden its sympathies and develop a fuller appreciation of the spiritual emphases of other traditions within the Church. There have been various factors within charismatic spirituality that have led in this direction.

(1) There is an inherent ecumenical breadth within charismatic renewal, surfacing, as it does, as a renewal movement in very different traditions. There has been much sharing and consequent cross-fertilization between evangelicals involved in charismatic renewal and those similarly affected within different traditions. I was particularly aware of this when I worked in an ecumenical community of Reconciliation and Renewal in

Northern Ireland. In a culture where most evangelicals were still asserting that a Roman Catholic could not possibly be a 'born-again Christian', the experience of being 'baptized in the Spirit' (in both Protestant and Catholic communities), immediately, and often painfully, changed that fundamental spiritual and cultural judgement. There emerges a greater openness to accept some understandings of the life of faith and biblical truth other than those previously sanctioned by one's own culture and faith-community. Certain beliefs and attitudes are no longer sustainable in the light of what God seems to be doing – at first it may be seen as a case of 'God breaking his own rules!' Soon, the tradition and scripture have to be re-examined in the light of these new horizons, and many formerly held convictions are discarded as blinkered outlooks which had been conditioned by particular views of religion, power and culture.

(2) Charismatic renewal has challenged an evangelicalism which, in some instances, has revealed an excess of cerebralism and legalism in its spirituality. The Report of the Church of England's Doctrine Commission on the work of the Holy Spirit expressed this thought in even stronger language: 'The Charismatic movement has been the vehicle of a true judgement of the Holy Spirit upon the moralistic and cerebral styles of evangelical piety.'[9] While charismatic spirituality is not, in essence, non-rational, it does provide a way of exploring the non-rational within spirituality (and therefore the personality in general). For instance, the gift of tongues can be seen as a symbol of the non-rational elements within spirituality. It claims that, for a time, it is possible to leave aside the control of the rational intellect in prayer and worship, and communicate with God directly from the heart, with that part of one's being that is not subject to one's rational control. St Paul, in his day, spoke of praying with the mind, and praying with the spirit. Speaking in tongues can be seen as taking risks and exploring new territory when relating to God in prayer and worship. The rational mind is relinquishing its direct and normal control so that the non-rational can become the vehicle of expression of longings and worship that are above and beyond the capacity of the finite and

[9] *We Believe in the Holy Spirit* (London, Church House Publishing 1991), p. 72.

limited ability of human rational expression. St Paul himself alludes to that experience in prayer which is beyond words and the ability of human intelligence when he speaks of the Spirit of God praying within us with sighs too deep for words (Romans 8:26). Charismatic renewal has thus re-opened, in a more urgent way, questions which have confronted evangelical spirituality all along: What is the relationship (or right balance) between the affective and the intellectual, the emotional and the logical, the ordinary and the miraculous, between Word and Spirit?

(3) Charismatic renewal exists within a broader range of spiritualities than has been true of traditional evangelicalism. This spiritual affinity with other traditions outside of evangelicalism is evidenced, for instance, in such things as the concept of worship which underlies the practice of singing in tongues, the place of picture and vision, and the centrality of the category of miracle and healing. Singing in tongues reflects an understanding of worship which is far nearer the Eastern Christian tradition than the Western. It is an expression of the less word-dominated, less time-conscious approach to worship, where the central concern is to enter into the activity of the hosts of heaven, where articulation and verbal expression are less crucial than in most Western traditions of worship. The receiving of 'pictures from the Lord', both in private prayer and in corporate worship, which is an almost universal feature of charismatic renewal, links again much more easily with the Orthodox tradition which gives an importance to the place of the visual in prayer, through the central place of icons within that tradition, and with the experience of visions which have been a feature of the Western (Roman) Catholic tradition. The charismatic emphasis on healing again provides many more points of contact with a catholic emphasis on healing than with traditional evangelicalism where the healing ministry has played a much less significant part. Each of these bridges of spiritual perception have opened up new routes into different historical traditions of spirituality for those sections of evangelicalism that have assimilated the emphases of charismatic spirituality.

(4) This opening of new windows on other worlds has been accompanied by a reworking of various biblical and doctrinal definitions, hitherto widely accepted within evangelicalism. The

view that the *charismata* mentioned by Paul in his Corinthian correspondence were confined to the experience of the New Testament period only has been one of the most obvious to have been challenged by the new experience of charismatic phenomena; the doctrinal positions which drew a specific line between the New Testament period and the subsequent ages of the Church have been abandoned by the majority of evangelicals, such that they now accept that the spirituality of the New Testament (whatever may be our difficulties in understanding and describing exactly what that is) is the common inheritance of all Christians from the time of Christ to the end of the age.

The greatest doctrinal challenge has come in the whole area of the way in which the Holy Spirit is perceived as coming to an individual. This has not been resolved in any simple way at all, and now a wide diversity of understandings of 'the coming(s) of the Spirit' prevail throughout evangelicalism. In the evangelical concern for truth there has been the belief that the work of the Spirit can be defined with an accuracy and precision that human language can encapsulate. Many evangelical charismatics have wanted to be similarly prescriptive in the way they explain their renewal experience of the Spirit; consequently the discussions continue over what is meant by the promise of Jesus that he will baptize his followers with the Holy Spirit. Some hold that this is an experience subsequent to and additional to new birth and conversion; yet others, who recognize its importance, see it as the conscious appropriation of something that has always been true of every Christian. The debate continues, though the process has probably alerted many to the truth attested by John V. Taylor:

> The authenticity of the Book of the Acts is gloriously apparent in the inconsistency of the various incidents of the Spirit's intervention from the Day of Pentecost onwards . . . Shocking theology! . . . The Holy Spirit does not appear to have read the rubrics! He will not and cannot be bound. Christians, on the other hand, put on a sorry display of special pleading and dishonest handling of the evidence in

their efforts to harness his freedom to their particular family coach.[10]

Watchman Nee, the influential Chinese evangelical, develops this in relation to the particular concerns of evangelical spirituality:

> When the Holy Spirit is poured out upon God's people their experiences will differ widely. Some will receive new vision, others will know a new liberty in soul-winning, others will proclaim the Word of God with fresh power, and yet others will be filled with heavenly joy or overflowing praise ... There is nothing stereotyped about God's dealings with his children. Therefore we must not, by our prejudices and preconceptions, make water-tight compartments for the working of his Spirit, either in our own lives or in the lives of others ... We must leave God free to work as he wills, and to give what evidence he pleases of the work he does. He is Lord, and it is not for us to legislate for him.[11]

While evangelicals have normally held a variety of views about the work of the Spirit, the influence of charismatic renewal has opened up a much wider spectrum which has, over the past quarter of a century, brought a significant increase in diversity – some regret this and long for greater precision of agreed definition; others see it as the inevitable result of the work of the Spirit who, while consistent, is not predictable nor to be confined within any human formula.

Evangelical Evaluation of Charismatic Experience

However widespread may be the assimilation of charismatic emphases into evangelical spirituality, and the consequent broadening of its horizons,[12] there remains a concern to evaluate

---

[10] John V. Taylor, *The Go-Between God* (London, SCM Press 1972), pp. 119f.
[11] Watchman Nee, *The Normal Christian Life* (London, Victory Press 1957), p. 93.
[12] There are, for all to see, some evangelicals who become more exclusive as a result of charismatic renewal. Often this is confined to the initial post-discovery period, as for instance, can be seen in some of the newer house-

the experiences in the light of Scripture. Most would accept the typical framework for such testing, given in the eighteenth century by evangelicalism's foremost student of spiritual experience, Jonathan Edwards.[13] He provided five tests by which to judge any claim for a renewing work of God's Spirit.

(1) Does it exalt Jesus Christ? (cf. John 16:14)
(2) Does it attack the kingdom of darkness? (cf. John 16:8)
(3) Does it honour the scriptures? (cf. John 14:26)
(4) Does it promote sound doctrine? (cf. John 16:13)
(5) Does it lead to an outpouring of love towards God and man? (cf. John 14:15–24)

For evangelicals, such tests are important because no spiritual experience is self-authenticating. The only sure test is conformity with the revealed will of God in scripture. Of Edwards' five tests about the work of the Holy Spirit, the first has been at the forefront as evangelicals have grappled with the implications of charismatic spirituality – does it exalt Christ? There has been a frequently expressed concern, by doubters and enthusiasts alike, to give due weight to the sentiments of John 16:14 – 'He will glorify me, because he will take what is mine and declare it to you.' In the last analysis, if any spirituality is directed to the glorification of the Spirit it is defective or erroneous. In this regard, an examination of the hymnody and worship choruses of charismatic evangelicals shows that the focus for glorification is Christ and not the Spirit. The Holy Spirit figures more largely in charismatic worship songs than in other types of hymnody, but this is largely in relation to his function within the individual and the believing community, not as the focus of glory and worship. Indeed, to preserve the exclusive rights of Christ over the Spirit in worship some have changed the words in some worship choruses that seem to be transgressing at this point. For instance, the third verse of one chorus begins 'Spirit we

---

churches which increasingly broaden their sympathies and vision. However, the strands of world-denying super-spirituality (to which we return later) are present in various forms of evangelicalism and charismatic renewal. When these meet and merge, horizons are often narrowed to a point of sectarian exclusiveness.

[13] Jonathan Edwards, *The Distinguishing Marks of the Work of the Spirit of God* (1741).

love you, we worship, and adore you, glorify your name in all the earth.' Some have changed this to 'glorify his name ...' (i.e., Christ's name), thus seeking to avoid all danger of giving Christ's glory to the Holy Spirit. While this reveals a commendable evangelical desire that no one should be led into error by singing anything uncritically, it could also encourage an over-hierarchical and subordinationist understanding of the Trinity.

The Leaders of Evangelicalism

In any description of the varieties of evangelical spirituality as they have evolved over the past two-and-a-half centuries, the views expressed by its leaders are clearly important source material. I quote from a wide range of them in the hope that the result will be a reasonably representative coverage of mainstream evangelical thought, piety and action.

To some, these people will be household names – Amy Carmichael, Samuel Chadwick, William Cowper, Billy Graham, Charles Finney, Frances Ridley Havergal, Roy Hession, Bishop Festo Kivengere, Martin Lloyd-Jones, Bishop Handley Moule, Robert Murray McCheyne, Dwight L. Moody, Watchman Nee, John Newton, Jim Packer, Bishop J. C. Ryle, Charles Simeon, Charles Spurgeon, John Stott, R. A. Torrey, David Watson, John and Charles Wesley. To others, many of these will be unfamiliar figures. They include in their number scholars as well as popular preachers with very little formal education behind them. They come from England, Scotland, Wales, Ireland, America, Africa and China. They cover a breadth of denominations including Anglican, Baptist, Methodist, Presbyterian. All of their views will have been influenced by their own personalities and their particular spiritual experience, as well as the culture of their age (whether they were mainly reflecting the approach of that culture, or more consciously seeking to react against it). All of these factors should cause us caution when we compare the views of one individual with another, and one age with those that follow or precede it, but hopefully, given such discernment, the essential unity (rather than uniformity) of the range of evangelical spirituality will be evident as we notice the developments which have taken place at different stages in its history.

To look again at the list of leaders who make up part of
the 'evangelical galaxy' quickly reveals that any discovery of
evangelical spirituality (even in its English Anglican forms)
cannot be successful as long as it confines itself to these islands.
The British-American link is an important factor. From the
initial influence of Jonathan Edwards from New England on the
leaders of the British eighteenth-century Evangelical Revival,
which was considerable, there has been a continuous cross-
fertilization, such that evangelicalism has probably taken more
from the developing American religious culture than have other
spiritual traditions in Britain – as, for instance, in the visits of
the Wesleys and Whitefield to America, the nineteenth- and
early twentieth-century revivalism associated with Charles
Finney and Moody and Sankey, the evangelistic crusades of
Billy Graham, and the American factor in the internationaliz-
ation process encouraged by charismatic renewal.

While it is difficult to over-emphasize the American influence
(because it is far more pervasive than most people on this side
of the Atlantic have realized, or would *want* it to be!), it would
be only too easy to exaggerate the importance of the leaders,
teachers and preachers within the development of evangelical
spirituality. They are to be seen as representative illustrations
of the theological, spiritual and cultural emphases of the evangelicalism of their age. They are more reflective than formative
of the spirituality of their group and generation; they explicate
the tradition of the people rather than form it.

A People's Movement

These leaders of evangelicalism must be seen in the context of
what has been, from the beginning, a people's movement, or,
in most of its manifestations, a mass popular movement. In
comparison with other spiritual traditions, it is less the creation
and evolution of the scholarly saint, the cloistered community,
or the aesthetic tradition of centuries of church leaders within
a particular cultural setting. It is a spirituality that forms communities of believers and, in return, is further developed within
these congregations of ordinary men and women. At times the
mass culture has been working-class, as with the great crowds
who responded to Wesley's preaching in eighteenth-century

Bristol; more often it has been at its strongest within the emerging middle classes; more rarely has it affected the upper-middle classes and the aristocracy; and that has largely been confined within Anglican evangelicalism.

A Spirituality that Sings

As a mass movement, with a spirituality often formed, to a great extent, by its members, evangelicalism has been particularly affected by social and cultural changes. For instance, since the eighteenth century, it has been in the forefront of the growing importance of congregational singing, and it has shown itself to be much more immediate in its response to the musical changes within society as a whole than has been evident within other spiritual traditions. Some outstanding examples of this absorption of popular musical expression are the adoption by evangelicalism of the music-hall tradition in gospel songs, camp-fire singing in its youth songs, and ballads and folk music in its worship choruses. Other spiritual traditions have often preserved an essence and ethos through their specific and traditional style of music; evangelicalism seems always to be changing the expressions of its corporate spirituality as its musical styles are, relatively speaking, so quick to change and adapt in keeping with the contemporary experience of its mass following.

This constantly changing and growing musical scene makes hymnology an important resource in charting the variety within evangelical spirituality. Since Isaac Watts, the father of modern hymn-writing, it has been a major factor influencing the movement's character and development. This tradition of congregational singing has, at times, been of the highest literary and musical quality; frequently adequate; and sometimes thoroughly undistinguished and temporary. Gospel songs prevailed in much of the nineteenth and twentieth centuries, with choruses for children in the early twentieth century, and choruses and worship songs for adults in the later twentieth century. Much of this is described as 'banal' by the musical and literary experts (as well as by those who feel themselves somewhat superior or sophisticated), but it is here that, often, evangelical spirituality is at its most vibrant and visible. This popular musical strand within evangelical spirituality sometimes arouses strong

emotional reactions in others – as with the somewhat dispro-
portionate fears expressed about the inclusion of some contemporary evangelical songs at a particular point during the
enthronement of the evangelical Dr Carey as the Archbishop
of Canterbury in April 1991. Most observers subsequently
agreed that such fears had been grossly exaggerated and proved
to be unwarranted by the event itself. In the pages that follow
we shall often turn to these hymns, songs and choruses as some
of the clearest available expressions of evangelical spirituality.

It is one of these popular evangelical hymns, a gospel song
from the last century, which provides the title for this book.
'Trust and Obey' was written by John Sammis (1846–1919), an
American Presbyterian minister. He was told of a testimony
given by a young man during one of Dwight L. Moody's missions in Massachusetts: 'I am not quite sure, but I am going to
trust, and I am going to obey.' He immediately wrote the chorus,
followed later by the verses. I could have wished to have found
a title in a more sophisticated poetic composition, one that
reflected a deeper theological understanding and exploration!
As it was, nothing else provided such a succinct pointer to the
heart of evangelical spirituality.

The three lines from this hymn which appear at the beginning
of each chapter will serve to recall some of the roots of the
tradition – popular style, personal testimony, American influence, evangelistic crusades, and individual conversion. It is
important to remember that its central concern with happiness
points to a stronger concept than the hearty jollity which the
word suggests nowadays. 'To be happy in Jesus' speaks, not of
some frothy emotionalism, but of a state of contentment and
rightness with God which comes through a commitment to walk
with Christ in daily living. For those, unlike me and many other
evangelicals over forty, who were not brought up on this hymn,
here are the words.

> When we walk with the Lord
> In the light of his Word,
> What a glory he sheds on our way!
> While we do his good will
> He abides with us still,
> And with all who will trust and obey!

> Trust and obey!
> For there's no other way
> To be happy in Jesus,
> But to trust and obey.

Not a shadow can rise,
Not a cloud in the skies,
But his smile quickly drives it away;
Not a doubt nor a fear,
Not a sigh nor a tear,
Can abide while we trust and obey!

... Chorus

Not a burden we bear,
Not a sorrow we share,
But our toil he doth richly repay;
Not a grief nor a loss,
Not a frown nor a cross,
But is blest if we trust and obey.

... Chorus

But we never can prove
The delights of his love,
Until all on the altar we lay;
For the favour he shows,
And the joy he bestows,
Are for them who will trust and obey.

... Chorus

Then in fellowship sweet
We will sit at his feet,
Or we'll walk by his side on the way;
What he says we will do,
Where he sends we will go –
Never fear, only trust and obey.

... Chorus

Popular Piety

In addition to its singing, testimonies to conversion and subsequent spiritual experience have always been an important part
of evangelical spirituality, as it is a piety of lived experience.
For many, 'giving one's testimony' is an important step on the
(unacknowledged) ladder of spiritual progress, probably coming
just before one's first spoken extemporary prayer in a prayer
meeting. Testimonies will also figure in what follows as
examples of the spirituality of personal conviction and experience.

Popular devotional aids are another resource when seeking
to put one's finger on the pulse of evangelical spirituality within
a particular period and cultural setting. These are the books,
tracts, daily readings, magazines, pictures, music cassettes, and
what might be called the minor accessories of the tradition –
things like stickers, lapel badges, Bible markers, greetings cards,
etc. These often give a more accurate picture of a people's
spirituality than do the books of its leaders.

Among the important popular influences on evangelical spirituality we must also recognize the significance of camps, house-
parties, conventions, rallies, crusades, and more latterly, holiday
weeks and Bible weeks. These have played a large part in
promoting intensity of devotion and new directions of emphasis
within evangelical spirituality.

In what follows it would be possible to attempt a description
of evangelical spirituality by describing and then evaluating its
various devotional practices, e.g., the daily Quiet Time, family
prayers (though much less widely practised today), prayer meetings, extemporary payer, especially intercession; but that would
be very unsatisfactory. It would be attempting to construct an
evangelical spirituality using a method that is at odds with the
very nature of that spirituality which is opposed to works, systems and methods. It sees itself first and foremost as a way of
life created by personal response to the gospel, or the grace of
God. Consequently, it is best described by focusing on the
cardinal doctrines and experience at the heart of evangelicalism
and then showing the particular spiritual and devotional attitudes and practices that derive from these; this is the general
approach adopted in what follows.

2

A TWICE-BORN
SPIRITUALITY

For the favour he shows,
And the joy he bestows,
Are for them who will trust and obey.

One of the surest ways of discovering the essential nature of a
particular spirituality is to locate its *creation-point*. In evangelical
spirituality this is the creation of new life by the Spirit of God
within the individual. In essence, evangelical spirituality begins
with conversion, when the individual responds to the gospel of
Christ. It is thus a spirituality of clear-cut beginnings. Robert
Murray McCheyne,[1] the celebrated nineteenth-century Scottish
evangelical preacher, left his congregation in no doubt of the
indispensable nature of conversion in evangelical spirituality:

> The conversion of a soul is by far the most remarkable
> event in the history of the world, although many of you do
> not care about it. It is the object that attracts the eyes of
> the holy angels to the spot where it takes place. It is the
> object which the Father's eye rests upon with tenderness

[1] Robert Murray McCheyne (1813–1843), in spite of his early death at the
age of twenty-nine, gives us one of the finest examples of the pastoral discipline
of the evangelical minister that lies at the heart of his own ministerial spirituality. 'Visitation notebooks record names of house occupants, family details,
illnesses, special needs. In red ink he noted the text he had expounded and
any conversation on spiritual matters. He was known to visit those who were
ill several times a day and made the dying a special concern. His notebooks
contain neat diagrams of the streets of the parish with names, details of families,
and even his prayers for their spiritual welfare.' James Gordon, *Evangelical
Spirituality* (London, SPCK 1991), pp. 123f.

and delight. This work in the soul is what brings greater glory to the Father, the Son, and the Spirit, than all the other works of God. It is far more wonderful than all the works of art. There is nothing that can equal it. Ah! brethren, if you think little of it, or laugh at it, how little have you of the mind of God.[2]

His congregation in Dundee may well have been unaware that the Bible offers different creation-points for spirituality. The prologue of St John's Gospel, for instance, gives a different starting-point from that which forms evangelical spirituality. 'In the beginning was the Word, and the Word was with God, and the Word was God. He was in the beginning with God. All things came into being through him, and without him not one thing came into being. What has come into being in him was life, and the life was the light of all people. The light shines in the darkness, and the darkness did not overcome it' (John 1:1–5). While these verses clearly influence evangelical theology in certain ways, they do not provide the creation-point for its spirituality. John's creation-point is cosmic in scope, taking us back to before the creation of the world, to the cosmic Christ at the centre of all things, who is the light that shines in the universal darkness to cast light on all people. Such a vision inspires approaches to spirituality that begin both beyond the created order and outside of the community of faith. We are in the realm of the spiritualities of the Eastern churches much more than the Western, focusing initially on horizons far wider than the creation-point in the evangelical spiritualities within that Western tradition.

In many Western catholic spiritualities the creation-point is the founding of the Church through the incarnation of Christ: the Church is the continuation of the incarnation and its divinely ordained life continues from age to age as succeeding generations are grafted into it. The reality of the Church on earth has an existence above and beyond the sum total of the individuals who make up its membership at any particular time. It is clear that any spirituality that sees either the creation of the universe or the creation of the Church as a fundamental start-

---

[2] A sermon entitled 'Conversion', preached on 8th May, 1842. *Sermons of M'Cheyne* (London, Banner of Truth 1961), p. 154.

ing-point will have a discernibly different feel from the traditional evangelical approach. The former envisages a broad process of the work of God into which the individual is incorporated through birth and baptism and in which the process of growth continues through faith; the other begins when the individual responds to the work of God's grace, and thus becomes a member of the community of faith.

A Spirituality of Radical Personal Change

While other spiritual traditions, for instance, will find their creation-point in the prologue to St John's Gospel, or in the call of Jesus in the Sermon on the Mount, evangelical spirituality gives pride of place to the teaching of St Paul about the radical discontinuity between life before and after the transforming work of Christ in the individual: 'So if anyone is in Christ, there is a new creation: everything old has passed away; see, everything has become new!' (2 Corinthians 5:17).

Speaking of his own conversion Paul expresses this radical break with the past, even though it was a history that he valued hugely, 'Whatever gains I had, these I have come to regard as loss because of Christ. More than that, I regard everything as loss because of the surpassing value of knowing Christ Jesus my Lord. For his sake I have suffered the loss of all things, and I regard them as rubbish, in order that I may gain Christ and be found in him, not having a righteousness of my own that comes from the law, but that which comes through faith in Christ, the righteousness from God based on faith' (Philippians 3:7–9). A whole world is now open which previously was unintelligible. 'Those who are unspiritual do not receive the gifts of God's Spirit, for they are foolishness to them, and they are unable to understand them because they are spiritually discerned' (1 Corinthians 2:14).

The New Testament text most commonly associated with this teaching in evangelicalism is John 3:3: 'I tell you the truth, no-one can see the kingdom of God unless he is born again' (NIV). It is at the point of this spiritual recreation, this rebirth of the soul, that spirituality, for the evangelical, begins. This is the basis of all that follows in the Christian journey and remains a central defining truth about a Christian throughout the whole of life. This is graphically portrayed on the memorial plaque in the Church of St Mary Woolnoth in the City of London, erected in memory of John Newton, the famous evangelical clergyman and hymn-writer of the eighteenth century.

JOHN NEWTON
Clerk,
Once an infidel and libertine,
A servant of slaves in Africa
was
By the rich mercy of our Lord and Saviour
Jesus Christ,
Preserved, restored, pardoned,
And appointed to preach the Faith
He had long laboured to destroy.
Near sixteen years at Olney in Bucks;
And twenty-seven years in this Church.

Newton had composed this epitaph himself, indicating what he considered the most important fact about himself – the radical change, the new beginning brought about by the grace of God in Christ. As a young man he had been a sailor who had fallen into a dissolute lifestyle and had become involved in the slave trade. At twenty-three he was caught in a terrifying storm at sea in which he feared for his life. In his desperate need he turned to God and cried for mercy. His autobiographical hymn speaks with similar clarity of this crisis point in his life:

Amazing grace! how sweet the sound.
That saved a wretch like me!
I once was lost, but now am found,
Was blind, but now I see.

In popular understanding this note of a totally new creation is often inextricably linked with two further factors – sudden conversions, and heightened emotional experiences. Neither of these are of the essence of evangelical experience, but both were perceived to be so within the nineteenth-century evangelical

movement known as Revivalism.[3] Though both sudden conversion and emotional experience have always had, and always will
have, a place in the spontaneous response of particular individuals in certain situations to the work of God's grace in their
lives, this does not make them essential to this new beginning
itself.

The radical nature of this new beginning is intensified by the
dire necessity for this work of God in the individual without
which he or she is utterly lost and eternally separated from
God. Augustus Toplady, another eighteenth-century evangelical
clergyman in the Church of England, captures the urgency of
this individual rebirth in his famous hymn 'Rock of Ages':

> Nothing in my hand I bring,
> Simply to thy cross I cling;
> Naked, come to thee for dress;
> Helpless, look to thee for grace;
> Foul, I to the fountain fly:
> Wash me, Saviour, or I die.

Without this new birth, the individual is lost, without God
and without hope. This brings an either-or quality to the heart
of evangelical spirituality, and ensures a lifelong awareness of
the critical importance of the new beginning: it is quite simply,
a matter of life and death. McCheyne, in the graphic language
of his day, emphasizes this choice between new birth and eternal
lostness:

> Dear brothers and sisters, all this hell that I have described
> is what you and I deserved. We were over the lake of fire,
> but it was from this that Jesus saved us; he was in prison
> for you and me – he drank every drop out of the cup of
> God's wrath for you and me – he died the just for the

---

[3] The main focus of evangelistic Revivalist methods were Moody and Sankey
who conducted several missions in the United Kingdom in the nineteenth
century. Their approach to evangelism, and in particular some novel techniques
and their expectation of instantaneous conversions, have remained a continuing
feature in most phases and varieties of subsequent evangelicalism. It is an
enduring example of the American influence. For a critical appraisal of the
ministry, theology and methods of Moody and Sankey see John Kent, *Holding
the Fort* (London, Epworth Press 1978).

unjust. O! beloved, how we should prize, love, and adore Jesus for what he hath done for us . . . But, O! beloved, think of hell. Have you no unconverted friends, who are treasuring up wrath against the day of wrath? O! have you no prayerless parent, no sister, nor brother? O! have you no compassion for them – no mercy's voice to warn them?[4]

Some have claimed that this note of salvation from eternal judgement is not a necessary feature of evangelical spirituality: it certainly occurs much less frequently in evangelical preaching today than in former generations, and the pictorial, spatial, and quasi-physical approaches have been abandoned. However, the general evangelical view is still that, when a thoroughgoing universalism replaces the understanding of the eternal lostness of individuals outside of Christ, then the emphasis on the need for individual conversion usually ceases to be a central feature in the understanding of the gospel. And, once this creation-point has been left behind, the spirituality has moved outside of the range of evangelicalism into another branch of the Christian spiritual tradition.

The weight given, in evangelical spirituality, to this radical new beginning is further emphasized by there being two separate foci at the juncture between the old and new order – the work of the Spirit of God in the individual believer (new birth), and the response of the individual in repentance and faith (conversion). It is at this point that one of the major differences between two types of evangelical spirituality can be discerned. There are those who put most emphasis on the sovereignty of God and the work of the Spirit in individual believers, opening their hearts and minds to respond to the call of God to repentance and faith. Others place greater emphasis on the individual's decision and response. The former is much more likely to find a place for baptizing the children of believing parents as a sign of the special covenant relationship which they occupy. They will emphasize the promise of the work of God's Spirit in bringing individuals to new birth in such a way that they will respond in penitence and faith – their decision will be a result of the unseen and unquantifiable work of the Holy Spirit within,

<hr />

[4] From the sermon entitled 'Future Punishment Eternal' preached on 15th July, 1842. M'Cheyne, op. cit., pp. 172f.

which was effectively affirmed in faith at the child's baptism. On the other hand many of those evangelical traditions that reserve baptism for believing adults only, emphasize more the importance of the human decision in the new beginning.

These two traditions are not water-tight compartments but do represent two divergent evangelical spiritualities. One emphasizes the new beginning as response, the other as decision; the former emphasizes the invisible work of the Spirit within, the second focuses more on the act of will and the individual's commitment. It is the second form that is most exclusively the spirituality of radical newness in the individual's life. The former has more space to give to the pre-conversion life of the individual, as already the sphere of the operation of God's Spirit. It is not, in essence, a distinction between those who do, and those who do not, baptize adults; it is the question of where the mainspring of spiritual life is to be located – in the prior working of God's Spirit or in the mind and heart of the individual. In practice, the emphasis on the individual's decision has been so strong that even those who practise the baptism of infants have given very little place to anything of consequence happening until the individual's decision is made. This has often meant that baptism has figured very little in understandings of evangelical spirituality because many who practise infant baptism do not see this as a significant work of God in the individual, and therefore, not one of the origins of spirituality.

A Spirituality of Redemption Rather than Creation

Matthew Fox, the American Dominican, who has been one of the foremost advocates of 'creation spirituality' in the Western world, issues the challenge to all of us, including evangelicals, who have been moulded within the Western spiritual tradition, to reflect radically on the basic shape of our spirituality. He has called for a fundamental revision of approach, what he would see as a rediscovery of a more healthy and relevant spirituality of 'original blessing'.

What religion must let go of in the West is an exclusively fall/redemption model of spirituality – a model that has dominated theology, Bible studies, seminaries and novitiate training, hagiography, psychology for centuries. It is a dualistic model and patriarchal one; it begins its theology with sin and original sin, and it generally ends with redemption. Fall/redemption spirituality does not teach believers about the New Creation or creativity, about justice making and social transformation, or about Eros, play, pleasure, and the God of delight.[5]

Though one might agree, in general, with his historical description of Western theology as fall/redemption rather than creation/original blessing, and see something in his critique which should cause the Western churches to think through many of the ways in which they have shown too little appreciation of these doctrines for ethics, discipleship, mission and spirituality, nevertheless the conclusions which would abandon altogether fall/redemption categories must be rejected as totally at variance with the teaching of the New Testament.[6]

This radical critique from the adherents of creation spirituality does, however, highlight some particularly strong features within evangelical spirituality where deficiencies have been evidenced at different points within its history. In basing its spirituality almost exclusively in redemption rather than creation, and in seeing this redemption more in terms of how it is applied and experienced in the individual than in its communal and cosmic significance, certain endemic weaknesses have appeared within evangelical spirituality. There has been, for instance, a recurring suspicion of various forms of art and culture, a reluctance, at times, to see creation, ecology and social issues as Christian priorities, and a difficulty in developing theological and spiritual understanding from any base other than the work of God within the individual.

[5] Matthew Fox, *Original Blessing* (Santa Fe, Bear & Co. 1983), p. 11.

[6] Matthew Fox is not content to see a spirituality that combines both fall/redemption and creation centred approaches – he asks for people to opt solely for the latter (op. cit. p. 28). While, in general terms, his characterization of traditional Western approaches to spirituality is helpfully suggestive, in the end he has overstated his case and painted a caricature of what is a much more diverse and inclusive tradition. While such an overstatement can be acceptable when calling for a new balance to be struck, it ceases to be of use when it becomes the foundation block in a full-scale realignment of theology.

A Spirituality of Renewal

Evangelical spirituality was born in a renewing, reviving work of the Spirit of God in the eighteenth century, and to the present day its most powerful and distinctive features are to do with the vitality of spiritual life in the individual and within the fellowship shared by believers in whom the Spirit has likewise been at work. Consequently, it is a spirituality which needs to be earthed within, and supported by, the broader historical tradition of the Church which is wider than the particular renewing work of the Spirit at any given time in history. As a spirituality of renewal, evangelicalism needs this wider tradition to save it from the excesses of individualism, extravagance and fanaticism, as well as from spiritual bankruptcy, should its own inner dynamic be lost. If a spirituality is no broader than the very essentials of evangelicalism it rarely survives well the transmission from one generation to another. This is probably one of the reasons (along with common rejection of parental norms and values) why so many children of staunch, but somewhat exclusive, evangelical homes seem to reject their evangelicalism in adulthood and turn to other spiritual traditions. It is because they are rejecting a package which was presented as a complete whole rather than as the inner renewing dynamic within a wider tradition of Christian spirituality.

To be a spirituality of, and in, renewal also makes it a very demanding one. To keep at the centre of one's discipleship the liveliness and reality of a personal relationship with God demands a daily life of obedience and openness to the work of God's Spirit, without which there comes a very quick decline into meaningless formalism, brittle cerebralism or petty legalism. This can lead some away from evangelicalism as too hard a road.

Whereas monasticism stands, for some traditions, as the epitome of the radical call of Christ to the few to forsake all and follow him, for the evangelical this radical call cannot be left to the holy and encloistered minority; it is the call to every believer. It leads to a spirituality of intensity, commitment and thoroughgoing discipleship. As such, some of the most authentic reawakenings of the central genius of evangelical spirituality have come from those who call for an ever deeper and more radical understanding of commitment and discipleship – and that, not in religious enclaves, but in the very fiercest places of the spiritual battle. It is the most noble strand within evangelical spirituality. McCheyne often reminded his congregation of the need for continuous renewal:

> The divine life is all from above . . . In some believers this life is maintained by a constant inflowing of the Holy Spirit – 'I will water it every moment' – like the constant supply which the branch receives from the vine. These are the happiest and most even Christians. Others have floodtides of the Spirit carrying them higher and higher. Sometimes they get more in a day than for months before. In the one of these, grace is like a river; in the other, it is like the shower coming down in its season. Still in both there is need for revival. The natural heart in all is prone to wither. Like a garden in summer, it dries up unless watered. The soul grows faint and weary in well-doing. Grace is not natural to the heart. The old heart is always drying and fading. So the child of God needs to be continually looking out, like Elijah's servant, for the little cloud over the sea. You need to be constantly pressing near to the fountain of living waters; yea, lying down at the well-head of salvation, and drinking the living water.[7]

McCheyne depicts a spirituality in which there must be constant attention to that inner spiritual vitality which needs to be renewed constantly by the ever-gracious gift of God's Spirit. In the contemporary Church this is an emphasis clearly seen in charismatic renewal. For a somewhat different twentieth-century example of this renewal within evangelicalism we could turn to Jim Wallis' call for a radically biblical understanding of conversion. He calls all Christians, and evangelicals in particular, to go beneath the personal and religious transformation of the individual's conversion to Christ and work out the far more demanding and painful levels of conversion that follow from the call of Christ as we allow this to challenge the particular social

---

[7] From a sermon entitled, 'The Cry for Revival' reproduced in A. Piggot (ed.), *The Believer's Joy* (Edinburgh, Knox Press 1968), pp. 112f.

and cultural situations which are so fundamentally at odds with the kingdom of God.

> We are called to respond to God always in the particulars of our own personal, social, and political circumstances . . . As such, conversion will be a scandal to accepted wisdoms, status quos, and oppressive arrangements. Looking back at biblical and saintly conversions, they can appear romantic. But in the present, conversion is more of a promise of all that might be; it is also a threat to all that is. To the guardians of the social order, genuine biblical conversion will seem dangerous . . . There are no neutral zones or areas of life left untouched by biblical conversion.[8]

In every age and culture there are those within evangelicalism who demonstrate this ongoing need for the renewal to be renewed. It is often a passionate plea that includes a critique of accepted evangelical spirituality from one, like Jim Wallis, who has been brought up within it. From his North American perspective he is a prophetic voice against the conformity of evangelical churches to the American way of life and the apparent success of evangelicals that has come from sailing along in the stream of modern Western materialism. It has led, he feels, to a dangerously low level of spiritual strength, concealed by a bright veneer of growth and prosperity.

> The gospel message has been moulded to suit an increasingly narcissistic culture. Conversion is proclaimed as the road to self-realization. Whether through evangelical piety or liberal therapy, the role of religion is presented as a way to help us uncover our human potential – our potential for personal, social, and business success, that is. Modern conversion brings Jesus into our lives rather than bringing us into his. We are told Jesus is here to help us to do better that which we are already doing. Jesus doesn't change our lives, he improves them. Conversion is just for ourselves, not for the world. We ask how Jesus can fulfil our lives, not how we might serve his kingdom.[9]

[8] Jim Wallis, *The Call to Conversion* (Tring, Lion 1981), p. 6.
[9] ibid., p. 28.

Wallis is speaking into the whole of Western (and not simply North American) evangelical and charismatic spirituality. His call is an intense challenge to a life of deep spirituality and personal holiness that is in itself, both individually and in the local Christian community, a sacrificial rejection and a positive Christlike alternative to an easy religious conformity with a sick Western materialism that has the seeds of decay so evidently at its heart. It is different in style and content from many other renewals within the renewal – but it is at one with them in the nobility and intensity that it evokes.

The Strengths and Weaknesses of Twice-born Spirituality

The practices that characterize a spirituality of radical new beginnings are more noticeably those which reflect a high expectation of what God can do in the individual, rather than his active presence within the community. It means that evangelicalism, to the consternation of someone like Jim Wallis, exhibits an inherent tendency to focus upon the inward and spiritual realm, rather than on society with its need for justice and liberation. It thinks primarily in terms of what *God* can do, rather than emphasizing the human search within the spiritual journey. It is concerned with invisible and spiritual graces rather than the tangible sacramental signs of God's activity within the Church. Its sphere of operation is the covenant of grace rather than the totality of human experience. Twice-born spirituality ensures that the more spiritual, internal and individual attitudes and practices attain easy and near-universal prominence, while other emphases find it correspondingly difficult to find their rightful place. They find doubts and question marks surrounding them – they are often afforded mere grudging acceptance, and, in extreme cases, are rejected altogether.

Spontaneity . . . Yes! Liturgy . . . ? Newness, spontaneity and reality are highly prized: they are seen as the marks of a spirituality that is personally valid and not merely a nominal adherence or cultural norm. Consequently extemporary prayer, both in private and public, is the dominant form of praying. It is the way encouraged and taught by parents, youth leaders and ministers. Just as one talks spontaneously with family, friends and acquaintances as a normal part of daily living, so extemporary prayer is seen as the natural and obvious way of entering into daily conversation with God. When not obscured by 'the language of Zion', nor descending into a subtle form of spiritual pharisaism, this ease and naturalness in prayer, both private and public, is rightly seen as one of the most important gifts that evangelical spirituality brings to the whole Church.

Such freedom often distrusts anything that is not spontaneous and, just as formal orations and prepared text play little part in everyday human interaction, so many see them as having little place in our relationship with God. For many, the use of prayers composed by others, and liturgical texts, will seldom, if ever, figure in their private prayer. Liturgical prayer sometimes suffers through being seen as a somewhat less real and authentic way of prayer. There is little sense of entering into the historical tradition of the Church's prayer, for someone whose life of prayer began with their own spiritual birth which is so formative for their whole spirituality. Also there is little appreciation of entering into the world-wide offering of the Church's prayer in the present, when the origin of prayer is seen to be the inward motivation of the individual, rather than the universal work of the whole Church.

Without such a place for liturgical worship as part of the diet of personal prayer, two other disadvantages can follow. The individual, with his or her particular interests, always sets the agenda for prayer, which can give a certain self-centredness to the exercise. Also, the lack of structure can leave one bereft when faced with a period of spiritual dryness, over-work, or tiredness, which, in themselves, often conspire against the ability to be spontaneous and personally creative in prayer – as in other areas of daily living. At such times prayer can disappear altogether if extemporary prayer is the only method used. Sister Margaret Magdalen, formerly a Baptist and now an Anglican nun, writes of the value of liturgical prayer which she has discovered on her spiritual journey (an experience that would be shared by many evangelicals as they seek to grow in the life of prayer):

There is a right monotony in such prayer. The one-tone of it does away with the constant need for fresh ideas, novelty and excitement. It comes to our aid very specially in times of great spiritual darkness and aridity when we can dredge up nothing from ourselves. There is a givenness about liturgy which enables us to jump into the great river of prayer that flows ceaselessly to the Father and be carried along in it even when we don't feel like praying. The Spirit can give life and liberty to liturgy when the heart longs to pray.[10]

While some incorporate liturgical prayer into their evangelical spirituality, the generally low appreciation of liturgy in private prayer among many evangelicals has its effect on public worship. Where the church tradition is itself liturgical there is often a desire, if not to abandon liturgy altogether, then to make it as 'real' and 'meaningful' as possible – betraying the feeling that, left to itself, liturgical prayer will be mere formalism. For public liturgy to be meaningful and valid there is often a major emphasis on the present and experiential engagement with the text. The minister, therefore, may go to great lengths to ease people into the liturgy, to introduce each section and prayer with remarks that enable people to enter into the prayer so that they can personally own it for themselves. This practice is one of the factors that adds to the wordiness of some evangelical worship – the antidote is an understanding of the validity and reality of liturgical prayer and a greater use of silence.

The spiritual and inward ... Yes! Symbol and sacrament ...? The centrality of the true source of a person's relationship with God must be preserved. Like Samuel, we so often look at the outward appearance whereas God looks at the heart (1 Samuel 16:7). True spiritual life and not outward show, religiosity, and ceremonial are what God requires. There has always been a welcome for the evangelical zeal of the prophets who thundered against the meaningless ceremonial of the Israelites: 'Incense is an abomination to me ... Your new moons and your appointed festivals my soul hates; they have become a burden to me, I am weary of bearing them' (Isaiah 1:13f). There have been times when anti-ritualism has been a seemingly all-consuming passion

[10] Sister Margaret Magdalen CSMV, *Jesus – Man of Prayer* (London, Hodder and Stoughton 1987), p. 81.

of evangelicals – for instance in the tussles within the Church of England following the growth of the anglo-catholic movement in the nineteenth and early twentieth century. Apart from these kinds of over-absorbing reactions there has usually been a robustly Protestant concern for the purity of true religion as inward.

There has generally been a concern within evangelicalism to preserve what has been seen as the New Testament simplicity of the service of Holy Communion. Often 'the Lord's Supper' has been the preferred description, emphasizing the gospel character of a simple meal of fellowship and thanksgiving. It is the attitude of heart of the individual and the congregation that is all-important – rather than the ecclesiastical status of the person presiding. The presence of Christ is more easily located within the fellowship of believers than in the elements of bread and wine or the eucharistic liturgy. There is a concern to avoid any view of the automatic dispensing of grace through the sacrament. Robert Murray McCheyne reminded his congregation at St Peter's in Dundee that there is nothing automatic about the grace of God:

> Doubtless, there are some children of God here, who did not find Christ last Sabbath-day at his table – who went away unrefreshed and uncomforted. See here the cause – it was your own slothfulness. Christ was knocking; but you would not let him in. Do not go about to blame God for it. Search your own heart and you will find the true cause. Perhaps you came without deliberation – without self-examination and prayer – without duly stirring up faith. Perhaps you were thinking about your worldly gains and losses, and you missed the Saviour.[11]

Evangelical spirituality has most often existed with reasonably infrequent celebrations of Holy Communion – monthly or even quarterly. This infrequency has often been intended to emphasize the importance and seriousness with which the worshipper should approach participation in the sacrament. Weekly communion has only more recently become a more common feature

---

[11] From a sermon entitled 'I Sleep, but my Heart Waketh' reproduced in *Sermons of M'Cheyne*, pp. 60f.

in evangelicalism (particularly among some Anglicans), though there have always been those who have emphasized the importance of a weekly service of the 'Breaking of Bread' (e.g., the Plymouth Brethren). Hardly ever has there been a daily eucharistic pattern within evangelical spirituality. The daily means of grace are pre-eminently private prayer and Bible reading which, for all practical purposes, are seen by most evangelical Christians as the most important and indispensable means of grace.

The personal and individual . . . Yes! The institutional church . . . ? The glory of personal salvation is the freedom of the individual to stand before God as his child, forgiven and accepted. There is no need for intermediaries, for Christ alone is sufficient to bring a person fully and freely into God's presence. The evangelical emphasis is more often on being saved from sin to become a child of God, than on being saved from non-belonging to becoming part of the people of God, a member of Christ's Church.

Consequently, there is often a degree of impatience with the idea of the Church as an institution. There is very little importance given to the Church's organization, its ceremonies or its orders of ministry – the priesthood of all believers is the main focus here. Often there can be an air of anti-clericalism about this kind of spirituality – and this is not merely the anti-clericalism of the rebellious pew, but one that can be heard preached from the pulpits. This can lead, in some people's estimation, to an undervaluing of some of the riches of Catholic order, but in its non-institutional character, and with its underlying hesitancy about the ecclesiastical establishment, evangelical spirituality maintains that note of freedom and prophetic critique which has always been a vital, if somewhat unwelcome, part of a healthy biblical tradition.

The believing fellowship . . . Yes! The local community . . . ? The individualism of evangelicalism, though evident in relation to the institutional and universal Church, is often counterbalanced by a strong commitment to the fellowship of the local Body of Christ – the congregation to which a person belongs. It is the local expression of the family of God that is the community focus in spirituality. It is often the quality, or otherwise, of that local fellowship which determines the balance between individualism and corporateness within a person's understanding of their faith. The sense of belonging within the local family of believers often involves an intense commitment to loving, supportive, caring relationships. There is usually a strong awareness of being a people of light in the midst of the darkness around, 'a chosen race, a royal priesthood, a holy nation, God's own people' (1 Peter 2:9). The commitment to each other within is emphasized by the difference, not to say hostility, of the world around. In the light of this distinctiveness of the fellowship within an unbelieving world, McCheyne urged his congregation:

> Dear children of God, unite your praises. Let your hearts no more be divided. You are divided from the world by a great gulf. Soon it will be an infinite gulf; but you are united to one another by the same Spirit – you have been chosen by the same free, sovereign love – you have been washed in the same precious blood – you have been filled by the same blessed Spirit. Little children, love one another.[12]

This commitment to the local fellowship as part of everyday spirituality can lead, not only to distinctiveness, but to distrust, isolation and rejection of the world and its culture. Conversion can lead to the ghetto; it can reject more than is necessary of the wider culture in which it exists, and with very little discernment and too few distinctions. It can produce its own super-spiritualized culture, replete with taboos and idiosyncrasies. Where this danger is avoided it can, and often does, lead to a strong missionary commitment. The love which it is called to express and demonstrate within its corporate life becomes one of the main strengths in its evangelistic vocation – the attractiveness of the people of God to those who know very little love, meaning and acceptance within their daily lives. Such a natural fusion of corporate spirituality with evangelistic effectiveness is a picture of evangelicalism at its best.

[12] From a sermon entitled, 'Thanksgiving Obtains the Spirit' preached on 24th November, 1839. *Sermons of M'Cheyne*, pp. 23f.

3

ASSURANCE OF SALVATION

Not a doubt nor a fear,
Not a sigh nor a tear,
Can abide while we trust and obey.

Within the closely interwoven family of Protestant spiritualities, the one element in evangelicalism which most clearly distinguishes it from its near relatives is the doctrine and experience of 'assurance of faith'. It is a primary feature of evangelical piety that individuals can be *sure* that God is at work within them. From this assurance of forgiveness and personal salvation flow so many of the specific features of evangelical spirituality. Without this certainty of faith at its heart evangelicalism would not have developed into such a distinctive tradition.

Blessed Assurance

If this assurance is missing then we have a deficient and debilitated evangelicalism. Speaking out of his experience as an evangelist, David Watson concluded that

> . . . through the low level of experience in much of the church, Christians today often lack assurance concerning their relationship with God or their forgiveness of sins. The result is invariably a weak and uncertain faith that, instead of shaking the world, will easily be shaken by it. In much evangelistic work I realize that some who 'come to Christ' are simply coming into assurance of their faith. They already have a true relationship with God; and in that sense I accept the accusation that I am often 'preaching to the converted'. But William Temple used to say that

'until a man is converted *and knows it*, he is not the slightest use to God.' Therefore whether an evangelistic event is leading to conversions, or only to assurance of conversion, is immaterial. Without assurance of the real thing, we have virtually nothing to offer God in terms of fruitful service.[1]

Assurance is seen as the necessary experience which leads to the dynamism so marked within evangelical forms of spirituality. For many evangelicals the world over, it is an experience most simply expressed in the nineteenth-century hymn by Fanny Crosby,[2] popularized through the evangelistic crusades of Billy Graham.

> Blessed assurance, Jesus is mine!
> Oh, what a foretaste of glory divine!
> Heir of salvation, purchase of God;
> Born in his Spirit, washed in his blood.

Whether sung in a crowd of thousands, or in a small chapel on a Sunday evening, the emotions of countless Christians have been touched, through this hymn, with a fresh awareness of the certainty, the thrill and the privilege of being a child of God. The nineteenth-century evangelical Bishop of Liverpool, J. C. Ryle, with the optimism of a confident faith mixed with a small dose of cautious realism, gives a preacher's account of this doctrine.

> The Word of God appears to me to teach distinctly that a believer may arrive at an assured confidence with regard to his own salvation. I lay it down fully and broadly as God's truth, that a Christian, a converted man, may reach such a comfortable degree of faith in Christ, that in general he shall feel entirely confident as to the pardon and safety

[1] David Watson, *Discipleship* (London, Hodder and Stoughton 1981), pp. 98f.

[2] Fanny Crosby (1820–1915) was more normally known by this name than by her married name, Mrs Frances Jane van Alstyne. She was blind from about six weeks after birth and married Alexander, a blind musician, in 1858. She was one of the nineteenth century's most successful writers of gospel songs in the USA, producing somewhere in the region of 9,000 poems, most of which are set to music.

of his soul, – shall seldom be troubled with doubts, – seldom be distracted with fears, – seldom be distressed by anxious questionings, – and, in short, though vexed by many an inward conflict with sin, shall look forward to death without trembling, and to judgment without dismay.[3]

In our own day, speaking of the way in which God's Spirit assures our spirits that we are children of God, Jim Packer considers that 'every whole-hearted believer who is not grieving and quenching the Holy Spirit by unfaithfulness, ordinarily enjoys both aspects of the witness, more or less, as his abiding experience . . . all Christians ordinarily enjoy it to some extent because it is in truth part of their birthright.'[4] There is more caution here than in other statements, but the continuing evidence down the years places the doctrine of assurance at the very centre of evangelical faith.

Puritanism: the Struggle for Assurance

To understand the full importance of the doctrine of assurance in evangelical spirituality we need to understand the meaning it had both for the seventeenth-century Puritans and for the eighteenth-century evangelicals, and to give full weight to the significant shift in emphasis that occurred between the two. It is this particular change that most clearly distinguishes evangelical piety from puritanism, one of its main parental traditions.

To the seventeenth-century Puritan, as well as to the modern evangelical, assurance of personal salvation was a key feature in their spirituality. In one of the famous works of this period devoted solely to this theme, Thomas Brooks leaves us in no doubt about the pivotal position of this doctrine and experience:

> Assurance is the beauty and top of a Christian's glory in this life. It is usually attended with the strongest joy, with the sweetest comforts, and with the greatest peace . . . An assured soul lives in paradise and walks in paradise, and works in paradise; and rests in paradise; he hath heaven

---

[3] J. C. Ryle, *Assurance: The Full-grown Faith of the Believer* (ninth edition, London, 1923), pp. 9f.

[4] J. I. Packer, *Knowing God* (London, Hodder and Stoughton 1973), p. 206.

within him, and heaven over him; all his language is heaven, heaven! Glory, glory![5]

The Puritans, as with most of their evangelical successors, were clear that one could be converted without having a sense of assurance, though this was, in some way, to miss the full benefits of faith.

> Assurance is not the essence of a Christian. It is required to the *bene esse* (the well-being), to the comfortable and joyful being of a Christian. A man may be a true believer, and yet would give all the world, were it in his power, to know that he is a believer. To have grace, and to be sure that we have grace, is glory upon the throne, it is heaven on this side of heaven.[6]

The very language here suggests that assurance is a rarer gift of grace than new birth itself. To be thus assured points to a Christian joy which is portrayed as an exceptional possession rather than a normal experience. It follows that it is not lightly given by God, or easily attained by the believer. The Christian who would attain assurance 'must work, and sweat and weep, and want to obtain it. He must not only dig, but he must dig deep, before he can come to the golden mine. Assurance is such precious gold, that a man must win it before he can wear it.'[7]

The picture is not of an easy faith, but of one that, though founded on grace, demands much personal exertion. To attain assurance was part of the struggle of the Christian life. A well-rehearsed exhortation in Puritan circles was 2 Peter 1:10 – 'Wherefore the rather, brethren, give diligence to make your calling and election sure: for if ye do these things, ye shall never fall' (KJV). Self-examination, to discern whether one was truly among the elect, was taken very seriously: 'Examine yourselves, whether ye be in the faith; prove your own selves. Know ye not your own selves, how that Jesus Christ is in you, except ye be reprobates?' (2 Corinthians 13:5 KJV). It was an heroic, totally

---

[5] Thomas Brooks, *Heaven on Earth* (1654, reprinted London, Banner of Truth 1961), pp. 14, 139.

[6] ibid., p. 15.

[7] ibid., p. 24.

absorbing spirituality, that bred a certain seriousness of disposition. Its concern with progress and searching one's soul led
to the often assiduous practice of keeping a journal – a practice
nowadays associated with a more catholic spirituality, but one
whose strongest roots are to be found among the seventeenth-
century Puritans.

The heroism of this struggle for assurance finds its classical
expression in Bunyan's autobiographical *Grace Abounding to the
Chief of Sinners*. This work ranks alongside the greatest of all
spiritual autobiographies. It is John Bunyan's own account of
his personal spiritual journey, which is far more painful and
heart-rending to read than his allegorical exposition of the
Christian way in his generally more widely known work, *Pilgrim's
Progress*. He reveals the intensity and anguish of years of struggle
as he discovered peace and forgiveness in Christ and fought an
inner battle to attain assurance of his faith. He was a man to
whom everything was vividly real, even from the time when he
was first arrested by God to consider the claims of Christ. It
happened as he was playing a harmless game with a ball and
stick.

> A voice did suddenly dart from heaven into my soul, which
> said, *Wilt thou leave thy sins and go to heaven? Or have thy
> sins, and go to hell?* . . . I looked up to heaven, and was as
> if I had with the eyes of my understanding, seen the Lord
> Jesus looking down upon me, as being very hotly displeased
> with me, and as if he did severely threaten me with some
> grievous punishment. (para 22)

There follows a detailed account of the struggle between the
Word of God, the accusations of the devil and his own doubts
as to whether he was really one of God's elect, which, as a
strong Calvinist, was the way in which the issue of assurance
confronted him most acutely.

> Therefore this would still stick with me, how can you tell
> you are elected? And what if you should not? How then?
> O Lord, thought I, what if I should not indeed? It may be
> you are not, said the tempter: it may be so indeed, thought
> I. Why then, said Satan, you had as good leave off, and
> strive no further; for if indeed you should not be elected

and chosen by God, there is no talk of you being saved . . .
By these things I was driven to my wits' end, not knowing
what to say, or how to answer these temptations. (paras
59–61)

In this struggle between the human mind, the tempter, and
God's Word, assurance eventually seemed within his possession.

> This scripture also did now most sweetly visit my soul, *And
> him that cometh to me I will in no wise cast out* (John 6:37).
> O the comfort that I have found from this word, in no
> wise! as who should say, by no means, for nothing, whatever
> he hath done . . . If ever Satan and I did strive for any
> word of God in all my life, it was for this good word of
> Christ; he at one end and I at the other, O, what work we
> did make! It was for this in John, I say, that we did so tug
> and strive: he pulled and I pulled; but, God be praised, I
> got the better of him, I got some sweetness from it. (para
> 215)

There is relief for the reader as we see such evidence of peace
and consolation come to a soul that had struggled so hard. Yet
it was not a struggle that had finished, for the assurance that
he was one of God's elect deserts him again on the very last
page,

> 'Twas my duty to stand to his Word, whether he would
> ever look upon me or no, or save me at the last: wherefore,
> thought I, the point being thus, I am for going on, and
> venturing my eternal state with Christ, whether I have
> comfort here or no; if God doth not come in, thought I, I
> will leap off the ladder even blindfold into eternity, sink or
> swim, come heaven, come hell; Lord Jesus, if thou wilt
> catch me, do; if not, I will venture for thy name. (para 337)

But the catharsis comes in the remaining two paragraphs of
the narrative, by such a hair's breadth does he discover the
assurance at which he has been grasping for so long. Even so,
the ending is not a joyous shout; rather he breathes a quiet
confidence and expresses the longing that the teaching he has
received through these trials will be helpful for other believers.

It is the picture of a valiant struggle, so movingly portrayed in the song from *Pilgrim's Progress*.

> Who would true valour see,
> Let him come hither;
> One here will constant be,
> Come wind, come weather;
> There's no discouragement
> Shall make him once relent
> His first avowed intent
> To be a pilgrim.
>
> Whoso beset him round
> With dismal stories,
> Do but themselves confound;
> His strength the more is.
> No lion can him fright;
> He'll with a giant fight,
> But he will have the right
> To be a pilgrim.
>
> Hobgoblin nor foul fiend
> Can daunt his spirit:
> He knows he at the end
> Shall life inherit.
> Then, fancies, fly away;
> He'll fear not what men say;
> He'll labour night and day
> To be a pilgrim.[8]

This valiant pilgrimage is all the more heroic when we remember that, after a lifetime of such intense self-examination and anguish of spirit, the final verdict of the Puritans was that, although assurance was so highly prized, it was 'a pearl that most want, a crown that few wear.'[9]

[8] The version quoted is the original that Bunyan wrote. The more familiar version that is sung today as a hymn, 'He who would valiant be', is an adaptation by Percy Dearmer, first included in the *English Hymnal* (1906). Bunyan would not have considered his pilgrim's song an appropriate ingredient for public worship as, like most of his contemporaries, he used only metrical psalms in that context.

[9] Thomas Brooks, op. cit., p. 15.

Evangelicalism: the Free Availability of Assurance

The eighteenth-century evangelicals saw assurance as equally important, but their expectations about it, and their experience of it, were so markedly different that a new spirituality had been born. Gone were the struggles, the introspection, the casuistry, and the metaphysics that were so typical of seventeenth-century puritanism. In came a new lightness, for the evangelical's spirituality was of a sunnier disposition. It is in the Wesley brothers that we see most clearly the epoch-changing nature of the teaching about assurance. Writing in his journal for 25th January 1740, John Wesley records:

> One came to me in the evening to know if a man could not be saved without the faith of assurance. I answered . . . I never yet knew one soul thus saved, without what you call 'the faith of assurance': I mean a sure confidence, that by the merits of Christ he was reconciled to the favour of God.

It is interesting that Wesley answers the doctrinal query from the *experience* of his followers – what he had actually witnessed as a result of his evangelism. Wesley was a true son of the Enlightenment: he was an empiricist who proved his case by experiment.[10] His Puritan forebears would most certainly have answered such a question by numerous and demonstrable scriptural proofs, and though, on many occasions, Wesley did defend his teaching from the scriptures, he reveals, in his way of answering here, the shift from the old puritanism to the new evangelicalism. There is far more emphasis on experience, evidence and

[10]   David Bebbington (*Evangelicalism in Modern Britain*, particularly in chapter 2) argues that eighteenth-century evangelicalism emerged when it did and developed as it did, as a consequence of the Enlightenment. Because the Enlightenment has most obviously led to rationalism and a flight from religion, the usual view has been to see evangelicalism as a movement opposed to Enlightenment thought. Bebbington argues that the experimental, empiricist approach of Wesley, and, even more significantly, of Jonathan Edwards, is a thoroughgoing Enlightenment approach. It shows an acceptance of the fundamental principle of the Enlightenment that all knowledge derives from the enquiry of the senses; the evangelicals merely included in their field of valid evidences the realm of the spirit.

pragmatism. The Bible is still the test of all doctrine but it is now used in a far less systematic and analytical fashion.

For Wesley, conversion was a sure and certain work of which the individual was conscious. It was, unashamedly, an *experience* of God's grace available to all believers. His own description of his conversion in the Aldersgate chapel on 24th May, 1738, conveys well the experiential nature of assurance that was frequently a deeply emotional conviction: 'I felt my heart strangely warmed. I felt I did trust in Christ, Christ alone for salvation; and an assurance was given me that he had taken away *my* sins, even *mine* and saved *me* from the law of sin and death.' It has long been debated whether this spiritual experience should be called his conversion. Most scholars now are content to call it that, as Wesley himself did, with the realization that, for many months prior to this event, he underwent much heart-searching and theological questioning which prepared him for this change. In looking through his journal some years later, Wesley added a footnote explaining that, before this experience, his faith was that of a servant; it was now the faith of a son. He clearly entered into the assurance of a personal relationship with God in which he discovered an experience of forgiveness and sonship that revolutionized his life and ministry.

This experience of assurance brought a new simplicity and, for the most part, an untroubled spirituality to the early evangelicals.[11] It was an experience which figured as a major theme in Charles Wesley's hymns from the beginning. The first verse of 'And can it be' (written within a year of Charles's evangelical

---

[11] There are occasional evidences of a continuing anguish within John Wesley, but they are rare and seem soon replaced by a sense of assurance. He had struggles about assurance soon after his Aldersgate experience – and these returned on occasions over the next fifty years. An example of one of these times comes in a letter he wrote to his brother Charles in 1766, in which he reveals a mood of quite devastating doubt: 'I do not love God, I never did. I am only an honest heathen . . . If I have any fear, it is not of falling into hell, but of falling into nothing.' But in the same letter he shows how near is his confidence still when he says, 'O insist everywhere on full redemption, receivable by faith alone: consequently to be looked for now.' Henry Rack argues that Wesley had to rely far more on the joyous experience of his followers to inform his ideas of faith and assurance as his own struggles were much greater than has generally been supposed – see Henry D. Rack, *Reasonable Enthusiast* (London, Epworth Press 1989) pp. 545–50.

conversion) poses the question about personal salvation: Is it possible that such a gift can be given to me, and for me to know it? This assurance, clear and certain though it was, should never be taken for granted; never become a mere human possession; and never be seen as something that the individual has achieved. There is that continual note of wonder that this precious gift has been given by God, and at such cost.

> And can it be, that I should gain
> An interest in the Saviour's blood?
> Died he for me, who caused his pain –
> For me, who him to death pursued?
> Amazing love! how can it be
> That thou, my God, shouldst die for me?

The hymn goes on to describe the process of conversion. Sudden it may be, but there were often, as was the case with the Wesleys themselves, years of struggle preceding the time when the individual realized that the answer to all the anguish, guilt and doubt was to cry out to God for mercy and to trust in Christ. The experience of conversion leads to a confidence that the Rubicon is crossed; the great eternal transaction has taken place. There will be countless trials, maybe doubts ahead, but the future is secure – there is assurance of salvation:

> No condemnation now I dread;
> Jesus, and all in him, is mine!
> Alive in him, my living head,
> And clothed in righteousness divine,
> Bold I approach the eternal throne,
> And claim the crown, through Christ my own.

For the Wesleys, this assurance of conversion was an intense and emotionally charged reality. It was one thing to be assured that Christ's death on the cross was the effective atonement for the sins of the whole world, and they, in common with many others, had always believed that. But what made the crucial difference for the individual was the assurance that Christ's death has been applied to *me*. The phrase 'for me, even me', which occurs often in sermons, letters and hymns, captures the

heart and the thrill of this experience of assured salvation. A
year after his own conversion Charles Wesley wrote an anniver-
sary hymn, 'O for a thousand tongues to sing'. The passing year
had merely emphasized the wonder of what had happened. One
verse of the original eighteen, which is not included in modern
hymn books, expresses the heart of this personal sense of amaze-
ment:

> I felt my Lord's atoning blood
> Close to my soul applied;
> Me, me, He loved – the Son of God –
> For me, for me, he died!

This experience of assurance is a gift of God that results
from the inward working of the Holy Spirit in every believer.
There is a direct witness of God's Spirit that confirms this truth
to the individual. It is not something merely to be deduced from
the study of the scriptures, though it can be, and neither does
one have to rely solely on the evidence of the fruit of the Spirit
that will emerge as a consequence of new birth.

> The testimony of the Spirit is an inward impression on the
> soul whereby the Spirit of God directly witnesses to my
> spirit, that I am a child of God; that Jesus Christ hath
> loved me, and given himself for me; and that all my sins
> are blotted out, and I, even I, am reconciled to God.[12]

Moderate Calvinist Evangelicalism: Assurance of Future Glory

The evangelicals who remained within the Church of England
in the eighteenth century and beyond, shared with Wesley in
the new view of assurance which replaced the former Puritan
approach. Even though, like the Puritans, they were mainly
Calvinist, they largely abandoned the anguishing search for
assurance in favour of the belief that assurance is freely available
as God's gift to all believers. They differed from the Arminian-
ism of Wesley in that they believed also in 'the perseverance of
the saints', the belief that once a person is truly born again his

---

[12] *John Wesley's Standard Sermons*, ed. E. H. Sugden (Epworth Press 1935),
1:208 on the Witness of the Spirit.

future place in heaven is assured. This has been a belief held by many non-Methodist evangelicals who continued in a moderately Calvinist position. The classic statement of the doctrine of the perseverance of the saints is contained in the seventeenth-century Westminster Confession of Faith (chapter 17):

> They whom God had accepted in his Beloved, effectively called and sanctified by his Spirit, can neither totally nor finally fall away from the state of grace; but shall certainly persevere therein to the end, and be eternally saved.

It is more popularly expressed as 'once saved, always saved'. The problem to be faced by such a doctrine is: What of those who have been converted and then quite clearly abandon their profession of faith and all attempts at living a Christian life – are they still saved? In strictest logic the answer can be 'Yes'. Such a position quite clearly lays one open to the charge of allowing Christians to live how they want because their future is secure. It could lead to an antinomianism of the most blatant kind. The instinct of most seventeenth-century Puritans was to suggest that if a person so fell away then they had not really been one of the elect; it had merely been a temporary faith. Consequently, it was vital to gain an assurance that you were truly elect. The alternative was to discover that, after all, you had been one of those Christians who merely had the appearance of salvation. This was the root of their anguish. The eighteenth-century heirs of the Calvinist tradition largely abandoned that particular way of dealing with the problem. They returned to the more Pauline way of facing the threat of antinomianism raised by the doctrines of God's free grace. 'God forbid,' they would reply to the suggestion that Christians could sin as much as they liked because heaven was already assured. This view of assurance, representing as it does a more Reformed position, with a greater emphasis on the biblical and theological foundations by which all experience is to be judged, has often fostered a quieter, less exuberant spirituality of confidence.

The Opposition to this Experience

Teaching on assurance has always been rejected by some Christians as presumptuous. The Council of Trent had declared that a 'believer's assurance of the pardon of sins is a vain and ungodly confidence.' The criticism from many, following the eighteenth-century Evangelical Revival, was equally trenchant. They saw the affirmation of personal assurance of salvation as a fantasy of the deluded enthusiast.

But this experience of assurance was so fundamental to the Wesley brothers that they went to great lengths to teach the doctrine that undergirded it and to defend it against their many detractors. Apart from numerous sermons and letters from John dealing with this theme, there is one of Charles's hymns, among many hundreds that refer to the experience, that is a deliberate and orderly statement of the doctrine written in answer to criticism. In its five parts it deals with the doctrine itself, the difference between pre- and post-conversion life, an attack on the critics' lack of spiritual perception, the rejection of the teaching by intellectuals, and finally appeals to all to experience the truth for themselves. Such a long and polemical hymn would never find its way into a hymn book nowadays but the first part did survive within Methodist worship. It is in the form of a spirited defence occasioned by the question asked in the first verse:

> How can a sinner know
> His sins on earth forgiven?
> How can my gracious Saviour show
> My name inscribed in heaven?

The second verse rings out with credal confidence as the assembled worshippers reply with a certainty born of their individual and corporate experience:

> What we have felt and seen
> With confidence we tell,
> And publish to the sons of men
> The signs infallible.

These infallible signs are the evidence of what God has done

in them, for they were, like their leaders, John and Charles
Wesley, children of their times, empiricists who were happy to
build arguments on the evidence of experience. Two of the
remaining verses in this part of the hymn outline some of this
evidence of the work of God.

> We who in Christ believe
> That he for us hath died,
> We all his unknown peace receive
> And feel his blood applied.
>
> His Spirit to us he gave
> And dwells in us, we know;
> The witness in ourselves we have,
> And all its fruits we show.

In the third section, Wesley flings strong words at the opponents
of this teaching:

> Tell us no more, we cannot know
> On earth the heavenly powers,
> Or taste the glorious bliss below,
> Or feel that God is ours.
>
> So ignorant of God,
> In sin brought up, and born,
> Ye fools, be not so proud,
> Suspend your idle scorn.
>
> For us who have received our sight
> Ye fain would judges be,
> And make us think, there is no light,
> Because you cannot see.

Evangelicals have often been criticized for the cavalier fashion
in which they dismiss those with whom they disagree, and
although Wesley was only giving as good as he got, whenever
spirituality is defended in such a combative manner, its own
intrinsic nature can be subtly changed. For evangelicals there
has always been the danger that confidence in God's saving
grace should be seen as confidence in having got their theology

right. There have, no doubt, been many occasions since Wesley wrote so dismissively of his critics, when evangelicals seemed to others more right in their own opinions than sure of God's gracious gift of salvation.

Clearly there are still Christians today (not to mention non-Christians) who are critical of the claims about assurance of faith, though in our age it is more likely to be an unconcerned puzzlement. When asked, 'Has God forgiven you?' many reply, with a shrug, 'I don't know.' There would be even greater hesitation if faced with the question, 'Are you sure of your future in heaven?' It is thought presumptuous to claim too much for oneself. Surely, the argument goes, humility demands a certain reticence when making such claims; and should not a true appreciation of the greatness and majesty of God lead to some sense of doubt or caution about our relationship with him in our finitude and fickleness? William Purcell, in a sympathetic appraisal of Anglican evangelical spirituality today, recognizes assurance as one of its main features, yet one which many others find it difficult to live with.

> For many faith does not come by that route. They cannot answer the questions as to whether they are saved because they simply don't know, and are rather horrified at the enquiry. Certainties are not for everyone; there are those who cannot live with them, and feel shut out from the blessed assurance of those who can. These include the large numbers who are permanently seekers rather than finders.[13]

For all the tolerance of our age, it would be a pity if that were the last word on the subject for all those who are seekers by temperament, and that assurance should be seen as the preserve of evangelicals alone. There has seldom been one who more consistently trod the path of the seeker than Dietrich Bonhoeffer, yet he knew assurance and the confidence it brings, as he wrote in a letter from prison to a friend in 1944:

I am so sure of God's guiding hand, and I hope I shall

[13] William Purcell, *Anglican Spirituality: A Continuing Tradition* (London, Mowbray 1988), p. 87.

never lose that certainty. You must never doubt that I am travelling my appointed road with gratitude and cheerfulness. My past life is replete with God's goodness, and my sins are covered by the forgiving love of Christ crucified.[14]

Though assurance is the jewel in the evangelical crown, it should not thereby be seen as an exclusive possession of the evangelical treasury, for assurance is part of the rich inheritance of every Christian. When, however, as in evangelical spirituality, it plays such an important role, it affects the atmosphere of faith in a number of particularly distinctive ways.

A Confidence in God's Promises

One of the effects of assurance upon a Christian is that 'he believes the Lord Jesus means what he says, and *takes him at his word*, Assurance after all is no more than a *full-grown faith*; a masculine faith that grasps Christ's promise with both hands, – a faith that argues like the good centurion, If the Lord *speak the word only*, I am healed. Wherefore then should I doubt?' asked Bishop Ryle.[15] A Christian has discovered the truths of the scriptures internally and is convinced by experience as well as theology that God 'has given us very great and precious promises' (2 Peter 1:4). Charles Simeon preached of this confidence in God's promises:

> Who can declare a thousandth part of the joy which a weary and heavy-laden sinner experiences in applying to his soul the promises of the gospel? With what avidity does he devour them! They are like the very first ripe fig which in the early spring a traveller sees and devours ere any one, however near to him, has time to claim it. And the man who knows not this by his own sweet experience has yet to learn what be the very first principles of the oracles of God.[16]

[14] Dietrich Bonhoeffer, *Letters and Papers from Prison* (London, Collins Fontana 1959), p. 87.

[15] J. C. Ryle, op. cit., p. 16.

[16] Charles Simeon, from a sermon entitled, 'The Word of God Precious' printed in *Let Wisdom Judge*, ed. Arthur Pollard (London, IVF 1959), p. 172.

Max Warren, one of Simeon's twentieth-century successors as vicar at Holy Trinity, Cambridge, described his experience of assurance as 'quite simply, a day-by-day, deliberate reliance on the promises of God.'[17] There is an awareness that, as God's Word is eternally true and valid, its promises are more to be relied upon than the seemingly contradictory evidence that may be a feature of present circumstances. For instance, the following verse has often been the bridge over which a Christian has crossed a particularly trying time in their life: 'No temptation has seized you except what is common to man. And God is faithful; he will not let you be tempted beyond what you can bear. But when you are tempted, he will also provide a way out so that you can stand up under it' (1 Corinthians 10:13 NIV). To be absolutely certain of that 'way out', though its form is totally beyond view at the moment, can give courage and determination even to those who are apprehensive by temperament. From the very earliest days of my own Christian experience I was encouraged, like countless others, to underline such verses and learn them by heart so that they should become fundamental to one's way of thinking and part of one's approach to the demands and opportunities of daily living.

Preachers and devotional authors have often exhorted their hearers and readers to 'trust in the promises'. It has been a feature of assured faith that characterizes many popular expressions of piety, fostering the sort of sentiments expressed with bounce and rhythm, if not much elegance, in Kelso Carter's gospel song:

> Standing on the promises of Christ my King,
> Through eternal ages let his praises ring;
> Glory in the highest, I will shout and sing,
> Standing on the promises of God.
>
> Standing on the promises that cannot fail,
> When the howling storms of doubt and fear assail,
> By the living Word of God I shall prevail,
> Standing on the promises of God.

[17] Max Warren, *Crowded Canvas*, p. 213.

Standing on the promises of Christ the Lord,
Bound to him eternally by love's strong cord,
Overcoming daily with the Spirit's sword,
Standing on the promises of God.

Standing on the promises I cannot fall,
Listening every moment to the Spirit's call,
Resting in my Saviour as my All-in-all,
Standing on the promises of God.

Earlier in this century, the 'promise box' was a popular way of ensuring that God's promises had a daily place in one's life. These resembled a small chocolate box in size, containing a hundred or so small rolls of paper on each of which was written one of God's promises from the Bible. You were encouraged to choose one of these minute scrolls from among the honeycomb collection, read it and take it as a promise of God on which to dwell throughout the day. It may be, for instance,

In all thy ways acknowledge him,
and he shall direct thy paths (Proverbs 3:6 KJV)

And on the next day, perhaps,

Fear thou not; for I am with thee:
be not dismayed; for I am thy God.
I will strengthen thee; yea, I will help thee;
yea, I will uphold thee with the right hand of my
righteousness. (Isaiah 41:10 KJV)

The promise would be a recurring encouragement throughout the day; a devotional thought on which to reflect and meditate. To most of us today this seems a rather quaint practice – a kind of genteel Victorian parlour approach to the Christian life – but, in the end, it is one of those numerous popular manifestations of everyday piety that are so common in all traditions, and which probably do at least as much to shape a spirituality as do the most powerful sermons or the very best spiritual writings.[18]

---

[18] This practice of meditating on God's promises is to be distinguished from the somewhat similar practice of taking a verse at random, and out of context, and seeing it as infallible divine guidance – an approach which deserves more critical appraisal.

On a more substantial note, such confidence in God's Word also gives impetus to the practice of regular and systematic daily Bible reading. There is the expectation that God will always have something for the prayerful reader, be it some fresh truth to assimilate, a promise to accept, a command to obey, a warning to heed, or an encouragement to receive. Bible reading is approached with the confident expectation that God will make his Word live in the individual's day-to-day experience.

A Boldness in Prayer

One of the reasons for the central importance of 'asking' in the evangelical approach to prayer is that God is approached as someone about whom you can be absolutely sure. There is that confidence in God that encourages the boldness to expect great things from him. It is an aspect of prayer founded on the promises of Jesus: 'Ask, and it will be given you; seek and you will find; knock and the door will be opened to you . . . If you believe, you will receive whatever you ask for in prayer . . . If you remain in me and my words remain in you, ask whatever you wish, and it will be given you' (Matthew 7:7, 21:22 and John 15:7, NIV; cf. also John 16:23, 24).

God, who has given such a sure faith, is approached in prayer as the one who longs to give good gifts to his children (Matthew 7:11; Romans 8:32). This bold approach to prayer is sometimes called 'effectual prayer', 'prevailing prayer' or 'the prayer of faith', and has been the subject of countless books about prayer. One of the most notable exponents of this emphasis was Charles Finney, the nineteenth-century American evangelist, known as 'the Apostle of Revivals'. A few extracts from his highly influential work, *Lectures on Revivals of Religion*, give the flavour of this approach:

> Prevailing or effectual prayer, is that prayer which attains the blessing that it seeks. It is that prayer which effectually moves God . . . A man must have some definite object before his mind . . . A great deal of prayer is lost, and many people never prevail in prayer, because, when they have desires for particular blessings, they do not follow them up . . . A Christian may come up as it were, and take hold

of the hand of God ... I have known persons pray until they were all wet with perspiration, in the coldest weather in winter. I have known persons pray for hours, till their strength was all exhausted with the agony of their minds. Such prayers prevailed with God.[19]

Certain excesses have grown from this high level of expectancy in prayer. Particularly when the promises of Jesus are applied to prayer for healing in a too literalistic manner and without due regard to the total context of a biblical theology of suffering, sickness, healing and death, then harmful results have followed. When people are told to go away and live as though healed, when manifestly they are not, and neither do they proceed to experience such healing, 'the prayer of faith' has tragically become the delusion that ensnares.

But even without its excesses, about which most have their favourite horror stories, for many Christians, such confident approaches to prayer are strange and inaccessible. For instance, William Purcell is largely correct when he asserts that the general Anglican tradition (at least as we see it in England) is perplexed, or worse, by this approach. He reminds us of 'those who do not look for such direct response to their prayers. They offer them, and lay them down at the threshold of that still centre where God is, and abide quietly with whatever results may follow, even if in this life there may not appear to be any.'[20]

There is clearly much more to prayer than is covered by this bold approach of assured faith, but evangelicalism has kept alive an approach to prayer that goes way back to the earliest biblical tradition; the tradition which sits with Moses as he raises his hands in prayer for the battle to be won (Exodus 17:11), which pants with Jacob as he wrestles all night in prayer for God's blessing (Genesis 32:24–26), and which kneels with Elijah as his fervent prayer prevails with God (1 Kings 17:1; James 5:16–18). It is a vision of prayer which many from different traditions affirm, whether consciously or otherwise, when they join with John Newton in his famous hymn:

[19] Charles Finney, *Lectures on Revivals of Religion* (London, 1913), pp. 50, 51, 73, 54, 58.

[20] William Purcell, op. cit., p. 89.

Come, my soul, thy suit prepare;
Jesus loves to answer prayer;
He himself has bid thee pray,
Therefore will not say thee nay.

Thou art coming to a King;
Large petitions with thee bring;
For his grace and power are such,
None can ever ask too much.

An Energy to be Up and Doing

To be freed from doubt and anxiety about salvation releases one from the need to search and delve inwards. It leads to that characteristic evangelical trait of a spirituality that is always 'up and doing'. The assured faith releases energy rather more noticeably than encouraging reflection, especially reflection whose links to action are not immediately evident. (Philosophical reflection has never been a favourite pastime for many evangelicals!) While there have been certain quietist strands within evangelicalism, the note of energetic service has been one of the most constant features of its piety.

This assurance-generated dynamism was part of the Puritan inheritance: 'The assured Christian is more motion than notion, more work than word, more life than lip, more hand than tongue. When he hath done one work, he is a-calling out for another. What is the next, Lord, says the assured soul, what is the next?'[21] It is as though assurance adds an extra octane to faith. 'Faith will make us walk,' says Thomas Watson, the seventeenth-century divine, 'but assurance will make us run – we shall never think we can do enough for God. Assurance will be as wings to the bird, as weights to the clock, to set all the wheels of obedience running'.[22]

The most noticeable manifestation of this energy is the commitment to evangelism, (see further, chapter 7) so evident in the style set by John Wesley: he always needed to be on the go and sharing the good news that had so changed his own life.

[21] Thomas Brooks, op. cit., p. 146.
[22] Thomas Watson, *A Body of Divinity* (1692; reprinted London, Banner of Truth 1965), p. 253.

He led a life driven by incredible energy; it is said that he did not begin to feel old until he was eighty-five. He has been aptly described as 'a lifelong vagabond in the service of his gospel'.[23] His was a spirituality that was on the look-out for results, and most particularly, the results of more people won for Christ.

All too often, this result-orientated activistic spirituality has led, paradoxically for the evangelical, into a form of Christian discipleship where acceptance by God is dependent on the amount of work done, the service accomplished, and the number of people led to the Lord. It can so easily rob the individual of the confidence of being accepted by God's free grace and, instead, lead to the treadmill of having to prove one's acceptability to God by being an over-active and successful servant of the gospel. While this problem is by no means confined to evangelicals, it is ironic when it dominates the life of one whose basic belief and starting-point is in salvation by grace alone, through faith alone.

A Present Experience of the Spirit

At the heart of the doctrine of assurance is an experience of God's Spirit which accompanies his inner witness within the believer: 'For you did not receive a spirit of slavery to fall back into fear, but you have received a spirit of adoption. When we cry, "Abba! Father!" it is that very Spirit bearing witness with our spirit that we are children of God' (Romans 8:15, 16).

John Wesley spoke of this work of the Holy Spirit as an inward impression on the soul that gives an immediate and direct awareness of God at work within. To have such a direct experience of the Spirit pointing to the heart of our faith, our adoption as children of God, gives depth and content to assurance. It brings freedom from being crippled by a sense of unworthiness, aloneness and littleness; instead there is the assurance of acceptance, belonging and significance. The possession of assurance is not dependent on accepting someone else's word for it, or even solely believing it because the Bible affirms it, but it is confirmed by the evidence of the dynamic witness of the Spirit within.

[23] R. A. Knox, *Enthusiasm* (Oxford 1950), p. 423.

When evangelical spirituality begins to lower its expectations of the Spirit, it is left assenting to doctrines, and living a life based on certain truths and experiences, while exhibiting a credibility gap between what is professed and what is experienced. It is the 'second generation syndrome', so common in renewal movements. When the ministry of the Spirit within the individual is less clearly taught, applied and appreciated, there is a dilution of the full-blooded content of the evangelical doctrine of assurance. It is possible that this kind of reduced expectancy has been one of the factors which has led many evangelicals to take the new wine of charismatic renewal so enthusiastically into their system.

By the middle years of this century assurance of salvation had become more a doctrine to be taught than an experience to be encouraged. It had become more common to teach people the facts on which assurance is based than to encourage them also to seek the inner and direct witness of the Spirit, as the Puritans and their evangelical forebears had done. We can see this tendency displayed in the teaching that was assimilated by young people from the earliest years of their spiritual formation. From the 1920s to the 1960s one of the main spiritual resources for children and young people within evangelical circles were the three CSSM chorus books.[24] In so far as these reflect the teaching and expectations about the Holy Spirit that children and young people were receiving, they point to a meagre diet. Assurance of salvation is clearly taught throughout all three books spanning the half-century of their influence, but in all the 709 choruses the Holy Spirit is noticeable by his virtual absence. Of the fifty-eight choruses on 'Assurance and Certainty' only two contain any reference to the Spirit, and that only in passing, and nowhere is there any mention of the work of the Holy Spirit in assuring us of our adoption as God's children. Furthermore, in the twenty-four choruses indexed under 'Sanctification' there is no mention of the Holy Spirit at all, and in the whole collection, the only chorus that deals explicitly with his ministry is 'Spirit of the living God', which

[24] CSSM are the initials of the Children's Special Service Mission (now subsumed under the Scripture Union), a highly significant movement encouraging evangelism and teaching among children. Its three chorus books were published successively in 1921, 1938, and 1959.

was adopted from the Elim chorus book, an explicitly Pentecostal source.

Likewise, in the two *Youth Praise* song books which were so widely used in the 1970s, while there is some increase in reference to the Spirit, particularly among newly written material in the second volume, the coverage is still comparatively thin. In both cases, the songs included were merely reflecting, in the mid-twentieth century, a lower sense of expectancy about the work of the Spirit than had characterized earlier generations of evangelicals.

Into this climate, in the late 1960s and early 1970s, the charismatic movement proclaimed the assured experience of God's love and power through the baptism of the Holy Spirit. Over the decades more and more evangelicals (and others) have discovered a new assurance by drinking this heady new wine of the Spirit. In some measure, at least, it seems likely that they were re-owning the fullness of the Spirit's work of assurance proclaimed by former generations of evangelicals. At this time, David Watson was one who enabled many evangelicals to assimilate the discoveries of charismatic renewal into their inherited understanding. He encouraged Christians to seek the fullness of the Spirit who 'gives an inward assurance about our relationship with God, a deep confidence that he is our Father and that we are his children . . . This is more than a mental acceptance of gospel truths. It is more than an intellectual agreement with doctrinal statements. It is a profound, inward, personal knowledge of the father-child relationship – a "heart-knowledge" that only the Spirit can give.'[25] John Wesley had been emphasizing the same, two centuries before.

In the wake of a fresh inner experience of the Spirit the gift of tongues was much to the fore. The initial prominence of this charism above the others mentioned in 1 Corinthians 12 and elsewhere was largely to do with its strange newness and sensational value; it also seemed to make an objective test between those who 'had it' and those who 'didn't'. At a more profound level it had to do with assurance; it was seen as added confirmation that the Spirit was at work 'in me, even me'. 'Speaking

---

[25] David Watson, *One in the Spirit* (London, Hodder and Stoughton 1973), p. 45.

in tongues is like a sacrament, an outward and visible sign of an inward and spiritual grace.'[26] As the experience matured, both in individuals and in the life of the Church, the gift of tongues has taken a less prominent place as just one of the whole range of *charismata*, and while these cannot be seen as 'proofs' of God's working, they are accepted by many as further evidential signs by which faith discerns the assurance of God's presence and activity.

A Confidence about the Future

Assurance about salvation *now*, gives a confidence to the expectation of heaven hereafter. If that assurance includes the belief in 'the perseverance of the saints', then all the more certain will be such hope. The Christian thus assured can say with St Paul, 'For to me, living is Christ and dying is gain. If I am to live in the flesh, that means fruitful labour for me; and I do not know which I prefer. I am hard pressed between the two: my desire is to depart and be with Christ, for that is far better; but to remain in the flesh is more necessary for you' (Philippians 1:21–24). There should be no sense of ingratitude for the gift of earthly life, nor a carelessness about the needs of others that would lead to a thoughtless desire to depart to be with God, but to know assurance of salvation releases death from the penumbra of fear, ignorance or confusion which is often humanity's experience at life's end.

Charles Wesley wrote the hymn, 'Jesus, the name high over all' in 1744. Years later, in 1781, he wrote, 'I have nothing to fear, I have nothing to hope for here: only to finish my course with joy.' And then he quoted the final verse of the hymn he had written thirty-seven years previously:

> Happy, if with my latest breath
> I might but gasp his name,
> Preach him to all and cry in death,
> Behold, behold the Lamb!

We see similar effects of a long-lived assurance of salvation in

[26] Michael Harper, *Walk in the Spirit* (London, Hodder and Stoughton 1968), p. 22.

Charles Simeon, whose last days were faithfully recorded by an anonymous 'constant attendant':

> On one occasion when I had bathed his eyes, and asked him if they were relieved, he said, opening them and looking up to heaven, 'Soon they will behold all the glorified saints and angels around the throne of my God and Saviour, who has loved me until death, and given himself for me; then I shall see him whom having not seen I love; in whom, though now I see him not, yet believing I rejoice with joy unspeakable and full of glory'; and turning his eyes towards me, he added, 'Of the reality of this I am as sure as if I were there this moment.'[27]

---

[27] William Carus, *Memoirs of the Life of the Rev. C. Simeon* (London, 1847), pp. 822f.

4

THE CROSS:
THE HEART OF
EVANGELICAL SPIRITUALITY

But we never can prove
The delights of his love,
Until all on the altar we lay.

Although the doctrine of assurance has played such an important
role in moulding the character of evangelical spirituality, it has
never been the major focus. Throughout its development, evangelicalism has consistently held to the same dominant and central theme – the cross of Christ. In this, it is at one with classic
traditional Western Christianity which has been marked by its
emphasis on the cross, whereas Eastern Christianity has much
more emphasized the significance of the resurrection. It could
be said that evangelicalism has simply held more tenaciously to
what has always been the heart of Western Catholicism.

St Paul established this primary evangelical mandate: 'For I
decided to know nothing among you except Jesus Christ, and
him crucified' (1 Corinthians 2:2). Charles Simeon saw, in this
verse, the touchstone of evangelical religion: 'In proportion as
any persons, in their spirit and in their preaching, accord with
the example in the text, they are properly denominated "evangelical"; and that, in proportion as they recede from this pattern,
their claim to this title is dubious or void.'[1]

There is no more important indicator of evangelical faith than

---

[1] Charles Simeon in 'Christ Crucified', preached in March 1811, *Let Wisdom Judge*, p. 110.

the centrality of the cross and, in particular, a belief in an objective atonement – that once for all, through the death of Christ, God in his holy love dealt with humanity's sinfulness and alienation, and reconciled the world to himself. The evangelical's concern is to invite all to enter personally, through faith, into the benefits of that salvation – great and free.[2] Nothing else in earth or heaven is as vital to evangelicals as the objective truth of the cross and a person's conscious acceptance of all that it offers as God's gracious provision for forgiveness, reconciliation and eternal life. Evangelical spirituality has learned, not only to live by this truth, but also to crusade for it, and, where necessary, to contend for it. 'The cross is at the centre of the evangelical faith. Indeed . . . it lies at the centre of the historic, biblical faith, and the fact that this is not always everywhere acknowledged is in itself a sufficient justification for preserving a distinctive evangelical testimony.'[3]

We Preach Christ Crucified

The cross has retained its central place in spirituality partly because it has reigned supreme as the concern within evangelical preaching. And in a spirituality in which preaching and the hearing of sermons is a central corporate activity, (see chapter 6), the place of the cross is constantly being reinforced for the believer. The cross is the subject *par excellence* for the evangelical preacher. Following St Paul, evangelicalism has placed the cross at the fountainhead of the preaching ministry: 'For I handed on to you as of first importance what I in turn had received: that Christ died for our sins in accordance with the scriptures' (1 Corinthians 15:3). One of the foremost evangelical theologians of the cross, James Denney, speaks urgently of the task of preaching Christ crucified:

The proclamation of the finished work of Christ is not

[2] At different times there have been those strands within evangelicalism which have insisted on the Calvinist and Puritan belief in a limited atonement – that Christ died for the elect and not for the whole of humanity. The predominant evangelical view, and the one increasingly widely held, has been that Christ died for all, and that the gospel should be offered freely to all so that 'whosoever will, may come'.

[3] J. R. W. Stott, *The Cross of Christ* (Leicester, IVP 1986), p. 7.

good advice; it is good news, good news that means immeasurable joy for those who welcome it, irreparable loss for those who reject it and infinite and urgent responsibility for all. The man who has this to preach has a gospel about which he ought to be in dead earnest. Just because there is nothing which concentrates in the same way the judgment and the mercy of God, there is nothing which has the same power to evoke seriousness and passion within the preacher.[4]

The aim of such preaching is not primarily to give information, but rather to lead to transformation, corresponding to the fundamental need expressed within evangelical spirituality – not ignorance and the consequent desire for revelation, but sin, and the urgent necessity of forgiveness. So such preaching must speak not only to the mind but also to the heart and the will. It cannot be content with enlarging the understanding but aims to lead to a life-changing response of the will.

In preaching the gospel the main appeal is to be made to the conscience, and . . . it cannot be made too soon, too urgently, too desperately, or too hopefully. It is because the atonement is at once the revelation of sin and the redemption from sin, that it must inspire everything in preaching which is to bring home to the conscience either conviction of sin or the hope and assurance of deliverance from it.[5]

Nowhere is this more clearly displayed than in the exotic Victorian pulpit oratory of Charles Spurgeon, the Baptist preacher.[6] As a preacher of great passion, Spurgeon reaches

---

[4] James Denney, *The Death of Christ* (1902, reprinted in London, 1951), p. 173.

[5] ibid., p. 167.

[6] Charles Spurgeon (1834–1892), the most popular preacher of his day, became a pastor at the age of seventeen. He attracted such large crowds that in 1861 he moved into his own purpose-built church, the Metropolitan Tabernacle, where he regularly preached to congregations of five thousand. Each of his sermons was printed and widely distributed. By the end of the century these had been translated into twenty-three languages and totalled over a hundred million copies.

the very heights of intensity when preaching on the cross of
Christ. He preaches Christ, and most particularly Christ cruci-
fied. In fact, without the crucifixion, Jesus is not effectively the
Christ.

> But where is Jesus apart from his sacrifice? He is not there
> if you have left out the blood of sprinkling, which is the
> blood of sacrifice. Without the atonement, no man is a
> Christian, and Christ is not Jesus. If you have torn away
> the sacrificial blood, you have drawn the heart out of the
> gospel of Jesus Christ, and robbed it of its life . . . As for
> me, God forbid that I should glory save in the cross of our
> Lord Jesus Christ, since to me that cross is identical with
> Jesus himself. I know no Jesus but he who died the just
> for the unjust.[7]

Not only is the cross preached as the central reality in the
Christ-event, it is also the touchstone of all Christian doctrine
from creation to eschaton. Evangelicalism has always been wary
of focusing on the life of Jesus in terms of Christ the Teacher,
the Example, the Prophet (important though these are as aspects
of his ministry). Jesus is emaciated if his whole life is not seen
in the perspective of Calvary. He is always the man born to die.
The cross is the central purpose of his coming, and the whole
theme of his ministry.

> To us the sacrificial death of our Lord is not a doctrine,
> but the doctrine, not an outgrowth of Christian teaching,
> but the essence and marrow of it. To us Jesus in his
> atonement is Alpha and Omega, in him the covenant begins
> and ends.[8]

Jesus as our Substitute

In emphasizing the centrality of the cross, evangelicals have
often been caught in considerable conflict over the particular
nature of Christ's sacrifice. Most evangelicals have wanted to

---

[7] Charles Spurgeon, *Metropolitan Tabernacle Pulpit* Vol. 32, 1886 (London,
1887) p. 127.
[8] Spurgeon, ibid., p. 128.

uphold as centrally important, that when Christ died on the cross he was doing so as our substitute – Christ died in the place of sinful humanity. He made the supreme self-sacrifice, freely and in obedience to the Father's will, without which humanity would be forever lost and condemned because of sin by the wrath of God. Because of this we, who are sinful and justly deserve the punishment of God, can be forgiven and restored to eternal fellowship with him. Christ drank to the full the penalty of our sin so that we may be delivered from the judgement that is rightly ours.

In Spurgeon's time it was becoming fashionable to denounce the doctrine of substitutionary atonement as uncultured, even barbaric, not showing a subtle and discerning enough under-standing of the nature of God and his dealings with humanity. Spurgeon entered the fray with considerable vigour (at the same time revealing his strong conservatism which often led him to prefer 'the old ways'):

> What a voice there is in the atonement! – a voice which pleads for holiness and love, for justice and grace, for truth and mercy . . . Do you not hear it? If you take away the blood of sprinkling from the gospel, you have silenced it. It has no voice if this be gone . . . If ever there should come a wretched day when all our pulpits shall be full of modern thought, and the old doctrine of substitutionary sacrifice shall be exploded, then there will remain no word of com-fort for the guilty or hope for the despairing. Hushed will be for ever those silver notes which now console the living, and cheer the dying; a dumb spirit will possess this sullen world, and no voice of joy will break the blank silence of despair. The gospel speaks through the propitiation for sin, and if that be denied, it speaketh no more. Those who preach not the atonement exhibit a dumb and dummy gospel . . . Shall we speak with bated breath because some affected person shudders at the sound of the word 'blood'? or some 'cultured' individual rebels at the old fashioned thought of sacrifice? Nay, verily, we will sooner have our tongue cut out than cease to speak of the precious blood of Jesus Christ. For me there is nothing worth thinking of

or preaching about but this grand truth, which is the beginning and the end of the whole Christian system, namely,
that God gave his Son to die that sinners might live.[9]

As Spurgeon saw it, many were in imminent danger of neglec-
ting the possibility of eternal salvation and choosing instead the
niceties and luxury of the latest fad of human wisdom. In the
light of eternity these fashionable hesitations about the death of
Christ as a substitute for us would be shown to be nothing less
than a passing delusion. Though Spurgeon largely avoided any
vulgarity in his exposition of the atonement, it is undeniable
that some preachers have often failed to do justice to the pro-
fundity of meaning in substitutionary atonement and have unwit-
tingly exposed themselves to the charges of being 'trite', 'barbaric', 'immoral' and 'sub-Christian', to name just a few of the
epithets that have been used against them. There have been
many examples, for instance, when the preacher has deserved
criticism in that he has misrepresented substitutionary atonement as a submissive, loving Jesus dying on the cross to placate
a stern and angry God in heaven. John Stott gives more reasoned
and cogent arguments in defence of substitutionary atonement:

> The essence of sin is man substituting himself for God,
> while the essence of salvation is God substituting himself
> for man. Man asserts himself against God and puts himself
> where only God deserves to be; God sacrifices himself for
> man and puts himself where only man deserves to be. Man
> claims prerogatives which belong to God alone ... God
> took his own loving initiative to appease his own righteous
> anger by bearing it his own self in his own Son when he
> took our place and died for us. There is no crudity here
> to evoke our ridicule, only the profundity of holy love to
> evoke our worship.[10]

But evangelicalism has not limited the cross to this one aspect
alone. Spurgeon believed that, when one had explained as
powerfully as one could the nature of Christ dying as our
substitute, there were other images to be added which would

[9] ibid., p. 129.
[10] Stott, op. cit., pp. 160, 175.

give the variety needed in preaching about the extent of what happened at Calvary. The cross can never remain merely a doctrine to be defined carefully, exhaustively and with exact precision. The cross is the central event both in history and in the life of the believer. Its benefits and the believer's experience of the cross are, in the end, so great as to be ultimately beyond human description. They certainly cannot, and must not, be trapped within the limitations of theological controversy, however vital such contention for the truth may seem at any particular time in the Church's history.

> The Passion is a great mystery into which we cannot pry. I try to explain it as substitution, and I feel that where the language of scripture is explicit, I may and must be explicit too. But yet I feel that the idea of substitution does not cover the whole of the matter, and that no human conception can completely grasp the whole of the dread mystery... The full, far-reaching meaning and result cannot be beheld of finite mind. Tell me the death of the Lord Jesus was a good example of self-sacrifice – I can see that and much more. Tell me it was a wondrous obedience to the will of God – I can see that and much more. Tell me it was the bearing of what ought to have been borne by myriads of sinners of the human race, as the chastisement of their sin – I can see that, and found my best hope upon it. But do not tell me that this is all that is in the cross. No, great as this would be, there is much more in our Redeemer's death... God veiled the cross in darkness, and in darkness much of its deeper meaning lies; not because God would not reveal it, but because we do not have capacity enough to discern it all.[11]

Whatever images one might add one upon another to describe what was happening in the crucifixion, its nature as a climactic event in which a divine-human transaction was taking place is paramount. The cross is to be seen as the event which decisively, and for all time, effected the possibility of eternal forgiveness: it is the irreducible foundation of the Pauline and Reformation

[11] Spurgeon, op. cit., pp. 223f.

doctrine of Justification by Faith on which the whole edifice of evangelical faith is constructed. It may well be that evangelical insistence on holding to a substitutionary view of the atonement as the essential meaning of the cross owes much to the need to preach the gospel in a straightforward way that leads to a response. An exposition of substitutionary atonement allows the whole mystery of the cross to be communicated in a manageable compass; the hearer is given a step-by-step explanation of the relationship between the eternal God, the historical event at Calvary, and his or her present spiritual state. The need for response can be clearly shown and the way opened for the individual to enter here and now into the benefits of what Christ did two thousand years ago. The cross itself, in all its richness, is less easily communicated as a simple transaction than some evangelical preaching has assumed, and maybe here, as elsewhere, evangelicalism has, for a time, lost a broader and deeper appreciation of the riches of the gospel through the exigencies of the doctrinal battles that have been waged over the years.

'This do in remembrance of me.'

The death of Christ is as central to the evangelical understanding of the ministry of the Sacrament as to the ministry of the Word. In different ways both the eucharist and the sermon proclaim the death of Christ and make it effective in present experience and, although the preaching of the cross figures more centrally in evangelical spirituality than eucharistic participation in the sacrifice of Christ, the latter has still a significant place.

For evangelicals, Holy Communion is first and foremost a memorial of the cross of Christ, but for most it is no mere memorial. Writing before the tussles between evangelicals and catholics about the meaning of Holy Communion, Charles Simeon defined the Lord's Supper as 'a memorial of the death of Christ and a medium of communion with Christ, whose body and blood we feed upon in the sacred elements, and by whom we are strengthened for all holy obedience'.[12] This definition

---

[12] In a sermon on Matthew 26:29 entitled 'The Lord's Supper' and reprinted in *Let Wisdom Judge*, p. 180.

includes the four essential elements most commonly present within evangelical eucharistic spirituality – the believer is confronted again with the awe-inspiring event of the crucifixion, enters into a renewed fellowship and identification with the crucified Saviour, receives the spiritual food of the body and blood of Christ as this is specially offered in the sacramental meal, and responds in obedience to him whose call is always to the way of the cross. It is essentially a meeting between the individual and the Lord, a brief interlude in which the believer is refreshed, strengthened and renewed for the ongoing life of trust and obedience. It focuses almost exclusively on the cross rather than emphasizing, as in some other traditions, the celebration of the presence of the ascended Christ within the universal Church, or participation in the glorious festival of the heavenly banquet.

There are strands within evangelicalism, particularly in our age, that place more emphasis on the corporate note of the celebration meal; there are marked differences about the nature of the eucharistic presence; there are various views of the relation between sacrifice and communion; but central to all is the salvation of the individual sinner by the unrepeatable sacrifice of Christ on the cross at Calvary. Charles Wesley who, with his brother, had a higher doctrine of the eucharist than many later evangelicals, expresses clearly the heart of evangelical devotion while pointing to a broader vision of the eucharist which evangelicals often come to appreciate as they live within the broader traditions of the Church:

> Our hearts we open wide
> To make the Saviour room;
> And lo! the Lamb, the Crucified
> The sinner's friend is come.
> Thy presence makes the feast;
> Now let our spirits feel
> The glory not to be expressed
> The joy unspeakable.

The Cross of Jesus in Devotion

The cross calls for humility, and that, to many, is its offence. It is a recurring theme within evangelicalism that many fail to respond to the gospel of the cross because of intellectual arrogance and pride, a pride that cannot admit that we can do nothing for our salvation – Christ has done it all when he died in our place. James Denney, in addressing this issue, found himself defending the sentiments of the otherwise not very remarkable revivalist hymn, 'Jesus paid it all, all to him I owe':

> It is not always intellectual sensitiveness, nor care for the moral interests involved, which sets the mind to criticize statements of the atonement. There is such a thing as pride, the last form of which is unwillingness to become debtor even to Christ for forgiveness of sins. And it is conceivable that in any given case it may be this which makes the words of the hymn stick in the throat. In any case, I do not hesitate to say that the sense of debt to Christ is the most profound and pervasive of all emotions in the New Testament, and that only a gospel which evokes this, as the gospel of atonement does, is true to the primitive and normal Christian type.[13]

This sense of indebtedness to God for the sacrifice of Christ is the mainspring of evangelical approaches to thanksgiving, worship and adoration. It is in the rich variety of hymns about the cross, often more profound than the revivalist hymn so stoutly defended by Denney, that this evangelical devotion is powerfully stated. There have been few more formative than the hymn written by the great Olney poet, William Cowper, in 1771:

> There is a fountain filled with blood
> Drawn from Immanuel's veins;
> And sinners plunged beneath that flood,
> Lose all their guilty stains.

Here, as in so much evangelical devotion focusing on the cross, there is an almost confusing intertwining of theological

---

[13] James Denney, op. cit., p. 158.

imagery, metaphor and meditation on the story of the crucifixion. To someone who is unfamiliar with this cross-centred
culture it can, at times, seem lacking in discernment, even
overdone. For anyone nurtured within evangelicalism, there is
usually a well-tuned facility to respond in different ways to the
abrupt changes from fact, to symbolism, to words of powerful
emotion (though Cowper's hymn with its over-graphic use of
the idea of blood-sacrifice has a strangeness even to most evangelicals today).[14] Cowper based his imagery of the cross as a
fountain on Zechariah 13:1: 'On that day a fountain shall be
opened for the house of David and the inhabitants of Jerusalem,
to cleanse them from sin and impurity.' The hymn's opening
verse is a bold statement of this startling theological theme
whose imagery seems crude to many modern ears, but it
expresses well the total immersion into the cross of Jesus which
lies at the heart of evangelical devotion. The cross envelops and
encapsulates the whole of faith; it expresses the superabundant
grace of God which is able to save to the uttermost. No sinner
is so depraved, and no guilt so deep and real, that the penitent
cannot be finally and fully forgiven at the foot of the cross. The
imagery is bold because the truth of which Cowper was writing
seemed to him so infinitely vast.

The second verse mixes this potent imagery with both the
story of the penitent thief and Cowper's own personal testimony.
The strength of feeling ('as vile as he') reflects the anguish of
his own tormented spiritual journey.

---

[14] Erik Routley, the hymnologist, expressed the hesitations that many have
about this hymn: '*There is a fountain filled with blood* is a magnificent piece of
evangelical rhetoric that has done good to many in the six generations since it
was written. But that hymn is furiously attacked because of its insistence on
the Biblical imagery of the Blood of Christ; and it gives offence to so many
that even those, who feel that a congregation that has grown into an understanding of its deep truth is better off than the one to whom the chance of such
growth is denied, know that they must choose it with the greatest care.' *Hymns
and Human Life* (London, John Murray 1952), p. 305. In *Hymns for Today's
Church* (London, Hodder and Stoughton 1982) the hymn is given a new lease
of life by a usable, but inevitably strained translation of the first verse: 'There
is a fountain opened wide/where life and hope begin;/for Christ the Lord was
crucified/to cleanse us from our sin.' The poetry has lost the power of Cowper's
verse, but the sentiment is more accessible to modern congregations.

> The dying thief rejoiced to see
> That fountain in his day;
> And there have I, as vile as he,
> Wash'd all my sins away.

The cross is so powerfully evocative that the poet invites us to enter with him into the story of Calvary itself and experience the very same words of acceptance as did the dying thief. Evangelical spirituality, though often wary of physical representations of the crucifixion, gives much place to picturing the scene itself and dramatically entering into it as a way of personal response.

In the third verse the poet, in his mind's eye, addresses the dying Lamb of God with words of confident faith in the universal and eternal power of the atoning blood:

> Dear dying Lamb, thy precious blood
> Shall never lose its power
> Till all the ransomed Church of God
> Be saved, to sin no more.

The power of the cross, or 'the power of the blood' has been a recurring theme in evangelicalism. However grave the sin, however dark the sense of lostness and depravity, there is no one too far away to be reached by the love and mercy of God, and to be justified by grace, through faith in the crucified Son of God. The converted drunkard, criminal, prostitute, witch, drug addict and the like, who have often given their testimonies on evangelistic platforms, or published their stories in pamphlets and books, are significant because they bear strong symbolic witness to the power of the cross of Christ to transform even the most obviously depraved or needy sinner into a servant of God.

The fourth verse of Cowper's hymn continues as an address to Christ and we are invited to join his response as he commits himself to a lifelong devotion to this theme which has gripped him so completely:

> E'er since, by faith, I saw the stream
> Thy flowing wounds supply,

> Redeeming love has been my theme,
> And shall be till I die.

Given his depression, this passionate commitment proved elusive in the poet's own experience, but it rightly expresses the burning devotion at the heart of evangelicalism. To be gripped by Calvary-love and to be motivated by it, is the very heartbeat of evangelical spirituality.

'When I survey...'

Just before the Evangelical Revival under the Wesleys, Isaac Watts had written what is perhaps the most famous and well-loved of all hymns about the cross, 'When I survey...' This set the tone for all its evangelical heirs in its combination of meditation on the story of the crucifixion with a powerful response from the worshipper, but it retained more restraint and objectivity than do most of the hymns on this theme within later evangelicalism. When we come to the nineteenth century there is a greater tendency to emphasize the powerful emotional message of the cross. This is seen particularly in the many female hymn-writers who were so formative an influence in Victorian evangelicalism – indeed it could be said that they inject a strand of femininity into popular evangelical devotion which counterbalances the somewhat masculine spirit that pervades evangelical approaches to Christian service and action.

One of the best known and most influential of these hymns of devotion to Jesus is 'Just as I am...' by Charlotte Elliott (1789–1871). According to Julian's *Dictionary of Hymnology* this hymn 'ranks with the finest hymns in the English language.'[15] It arose out of Miss Elliott's own personal experience. In 1822, during a time of spiritual uncertainty, she asked a German evangelist, Dr Cesar Malan, who was staying at the time in her family home, how she could come to Christ. He replied, 'Come to him just as you are.' She based her response to God on this advice and found peace and joy in a personal relationship with Christ. Twelve years later, while housebound through illness

---

[15] John Julian, ed., *A Dictionary of Hymnology* (London, John Murray 1892), p. 609.

(she was an invalid for the last fifty years of her life), she wondered whether she could still be of service to her Lord. The words that led to her conversion came to mind – 'Come to him just as you are.' That afternoon she wrote the hymn, based on this invitation, which speaks of the need to return again and again to Jesus who died on the cross where we find, not only the means of initial conversion, but also the source of grace for each succeeding step in the Christian's daily walk with God.

> Just as I am, without one plea,
> But that thy blood was shed for me,
> And that thou bidd'st me come to thee,
> O Lamb of God, I come.

And the central power of the cross of Christ is 'the cleansing blood' which brings the necessary daily forgiveness for the Christian to walk in the freedom of Christ. The second verse speaks of an intense awareness of sin and its consequences, which is cleansed by continual recourse to the cross:

> Just as I am, and waiting not
> To rid my soul of one dark blot,
> To thee, whose blood can cleanse each spot,
> O Lamb of God, I come.

This warm-hearted personal devotion to Jesus, the Lamb of God, together with the daily awareness of sin, guilt and forgiveness, puts this strand within evangelical spirituality alongside Roman Catholic devotion to the Sacred Heart of Jesus which has a similar feel and emphasis. That is a thought that would, no doubt, be unwelcome in many evangelical circles, but it emphasizes the universal and powerful theme of devotion to the cross in Christian spiritualities with very different histories, both theological and cultural. As B. L. Manning once observed, 'So in piety, do extremes agree: Catholic and Evangelical meet, and kiss one another at the Cross.'[16]

The step from such sentiment and emotion to sentimentality

[16] Bernard L. Manning, *The Hymns of Wesley and Watts* (London, Epworth Press 1942), p. 133.

is all too easy to take. It is at this point that evangelical spirituality can, at times, move from a healthy appreciation of emotion in religion to emotionalism, from strongly evocative doctrine to soothing and syrupy religion.[17] Though still worth defending as an example of a particular culture, the gospel song, 'The Old Rugged Cross', often steps over these unseen but vital boundaries – particularly as it has become a favourite of televised folk religion, aided by its catchy and sentimental tune.

> On a hill far away stood an old rugged cross,
> The emblem of suffering and shame;
> And I love that old cross, where the dearest and best
> For a world of lost sinners was slain.
>
> So I'll cherish the old rugged cross
> Till my trophies at last I lay down;
> I will cling to the old rugged cross,
> And exchange it some day for a crown.[18]

[17] The word *Pietism* is often used to describe emotionalism and sentimentality within religion. Historically, this term describes the seventeenth-century renewal movement within German Lutheranism which stressed the centrality of the new birth, a direct experience of God, and delivery from the power as well as the guilt of sin. In reacting against the formalism of the Lutheran Church of its day, it laid particular emphasis on faith, love, humility, patience, joy and the importance of mutual support through small groups of believers. There was a strong commitment to personal righteousness and social action (e.g., with orphans). Through its manifestation in the Moravians, this emphasis had a major influence on the Wesleys. As a tradition, it shows tendencies to emotionalism and sentimentality, which were some of the factors that led John Wesley, eventually, to react against the Moravians. It is quite unfair, however, to use the term, as is common, as a description of sentimental super-spirituality in general.

[18] This note of sentimentality was particularly evident in the Revivalism of the latter part of the nineteenth century. In the Crusades of Moody and Sankey, many of the hymns which Sankey sang used this device as an evangelistic technique, and as such it has been followed by most evangelists in the Revivalist tradition (like Billy Graham). The Victorians were much less cynical about sentimentality than we are. Now, to take a popular revival song, the famous, 'The ninety and nine' (*Sacred Songs and Solos* no. 43) would not have the same powerful appeal, especially the sentiments of the fourth verse, 'Lord, whence are those blood-drops all the way/That mark out the mountain's track?/They were shed for one who had gone astray/Ere the shepherd could bring him back./Lord whence are thy hands so rent and torn?/They are pierced tonight by many a thorn.'

There is the element of 'old-time religion' that permeates this song, making it part of that wistful sentimentality that aligns religion with the good old days. For all its personal references, it can so easily be a means of distancing the cross from actual history and vital religious experience. It creates a sentimentality that evokes warm feelings when sung (or maybe cynical dismissal!), but brings no challenge to present personal commitment. There seems to me an inherent danger in this, and similar, songs – though no doubt there are many who date their conversion from first hearing it sung!

The Cross in Daily Christian Living

The cross is not only the fundamental doctrine, the means of forgiveness and fellowship with God, and the focus of devotion; it also remains, through the whole of life, the motivating force in Christian living: we seek to honour God in holiness of living out of gratitude, and in obedience to the dying love of the Son of God. As an example of this spirituality of life lived under the cross, Amy Carmichael's *If* provides us with one of the most evocative expressions of the centrality of the cross in daily discipleship.[19] During the middle third of the twentieth century this was an enormously influential book in the development of evangelical spirituality. It held that all of life's motivation must flow from the cross. It is a standard seldom achieved but which leads to a way of Christian living that is, in essence, deeply intense: there is a deliberate self-consciousness to the whole of life for anyone who takes these sayings daily to heart, and there have been many thousands who have developed their spirituality around them. There are sixty-four in all; the following convey the intensity and earnestness of their approach:

> If I belittle those whom I am called to serve, talk of their weak points in contrast perhaps with what I think of as my strong points; if I adopt a superior attitude . . . then I know nothing of Calvary love. (5)
> If I find myself half-carelessly taking lapses for granted,

[19] Amy Carmichael, from her base at Dohnavur in Southern India, had a widespread influence through her many missionary and devotional works. *If* was first published in 1938. See further on Amy Carmichael in chapter 7.

'Oh, that's what they always do,' 'Oh, of course she talks like that, he acts like that,' then I know nothing of Calvary love. (7)

If I can enjoy a joke at the expense of another; if I can in any way slight another in conversation, or even in thought, then I know nothing of Calvary love. (8)

If I can write an unkind letter, speak an unkind word, think an unkind thought without grief and shame, then I know nothing of Calvary love. (9)

If I do not feel more for the grieved Saviour than for my worried self when troublesome things occur, then I know nothing of Calvary love. (10)

If I take offence easily, if I am content to continue in a cool unfriendliness, though friendship be possible, then I know nothing of Calvary love. (36)

If I feel injured when another lays to my charge things that I know not, forgetting that my sinless Saviour trod this path to the end, then I know nothing of Calvary love. (38)

If souls can suffer alongside, and I hardly know it, because the spirit of discernment is not in me, then I know nothing of Calvary love. (47)[20]

Expressing as they do, the powerful sense of sacrificial love which dominated Amy Carmichael's life, these sayings obviously and intentionally exaggerate the truth: to be guilty of one failure does not indicate a total lack of awareness in one's experience of the love of God revealed in the cross and poured out through the Spirit. But, given their poetic hyperbole, they reflect a sensitivity to sin, a gentleness, integrity and scrupulosity which demand the very closest imitation of him who gave himself totally for others. It may well be that such an approach to daily living comes easier to certain types of people than to others, but they are sayings with which few evangelicals would disagree. Some, however, have found them more guilt-inducing than liberating and sanctifying in their effect.

It is more commonplace now, than in former generations, for evangelicals to be aware of this guilt-inducing tendency in some expressions of their spirituality – and one of these is most

[20] Amy Carmichael, *If* (London, SPCK 1938).

certainly the continuing reference to sin that needs daily cleansing by the blood of Jesus. For those, and there are many of us, who all too easily accommodate ourselves to sin, and contentedly tolerate recurring failures in holiness, such an emphasis can be a healthy and necessary incentive to Christlikeness. To those who are over-sensitive about their sin, and even more to those who are prone to thinking that they have sinned against the Holy Spirit, (and that is a recurring fear in some people's experience), or to others whose self-image is so damaged that they are forever condemning themselves, such a daily coming to the sinner's place at the foot of the cross can serve to emphasize ever more strongly the personal sense of failure, even rejection. For them, a more appropriate form of evangelical spirituality would be one that focuses on the fundamentally evangelical notion of the 'once-for-all' objectivity of the cross, which assures them that 'there is therefore now no condemnation for those who are in Christ Jesus' (Romans 8:1). This is an emphasis particularly evident in some forms of charismatic spirituality.

All kinds of people can benefit greatly from a cross-centred spirituality, but one that is sensitively and appropriately interpreted to their own individual needs. The individual spiritual guide has often done this – and in the evangelical tradition there has often been a great tradition of spiritual guidance through friendship, fellowship groups, and sometimes, most significantly, through a ministry of letter writing.[21] But for most, the interpretation has come through the sermon (which for many fulfils the role others would look for in a spiritual director), and this, inevitably, can give no specific allowance for individual diagnosis and prescription.

---

[21] John Newton stands out as one of the great letter-writers/spiritual guides. Many of his letters were published in 1780, in *Cardiphonia (or the Utterance of the heart)*, following requests from many of his friends, who returned their letters to him for this purpose. Speaking in one of his letters about the strengths of his own ministry, he comments, 'So far as I can judge, anatomy is my favourite branch; I mean the study of the human heart with its workings and counter workings as it is differently affected in a state of nature or of grace, in the different seasons of prosperity, adversity, conviction, temptation, sickness and the approach of death.'

The Cross in the East African Revival

The place of the fellowship group has, at different times, been an important means in encouraging a consistency of daily response to the cross of Christ. We find one of this century's clearest expressions of this in the East African Revival. This emphasis in evangelical spirituality is one of the few in which the Western Church has been significantly affected by a spiritual movement that has grown to maturity in one of the newer churches. In the middle years of the twentieth century, Roy Hession's writings popularized what was often known as 'Ruanda teaching'. He transposed some of the main emphases of this East African movement into a distinctive form of English evangelical spirituality and, for a relatively short time, it had quite an impact on parts of the English evangelical scene.

At the heart of this spirituality is an emphasis on brokenness. The main obstacle to Christlikeness is pride, the arrogant, stiff-necked approach to life that is seen as the central spring of all that is destructive of our relationship with God and with one another. As humans we show a distinct aversion to brokenness – the human will strongly resists submitting either to God or to our fellows. Nothing less than the cross of Christ has the power to assail these strongholds of human wilfulness. The Christian may well have submitted to Christ initially at conversion, but will find this the continually recurring emphasis in daily discipleship.

> We are not likely to be broken except at the cross of Jesus. The willingness of Jesus to be broken for us is the all-compelling motive in our being broken too . . . Dying to self is not a thing we do once for all. There may be an initial dying when God first shows us these things, but ever after, it will be a constant dying, for only so can the Lord Jesus be revealed constantly through us.[22]

The openness and oneness in fellowship that comes as a result of this brokenness affects our relationship both with God and with one another. There are probably very few other spiritualities in the history of the Christian Church that so focus on the Johannine vision of fellowship as the centrepiece of their

---

[22] Roy Hession, *The Calvary Road* (London, 1950), pp. 14f.

approach – 'If we walk in the light as he himself is in the light, we have fellowship with one another, and the blood of Jesus his Son cleanses us from all sin' (1 John 1:7). The work of Christ on the cross was not only to bring us back into fellowship with God, but also into fellowship with our neighbour. Indeed, at the heart of Ruanda teaching is the conviction that it cannot do one without the other. Consequently, if we do not exhibit vital fellowship with our brothers and sisters in Christ, this is seen as proof that, to that extent, we have not been brought into vital fellowship with God.

It is a spirituality which is intensely communal. Like the very early Methodists there is a concern for one another's holiness, expressed in terms of 'walking in the light'. Essentially, as life is lived under the permanent gaze of the cross, all sin and darkness will be exposed. In practice, human deviousness, even in regenerate believers, is prone to avoid the light, and thus it becomes necessary for brothers and sisters, gently and lovingly, to point out the faults of another – to bring them into the light.

> In a fellowship which is committed to walk in the light beneath the Cross, we know that if there is any thought about us, it will quickly be brought into the light, either in brokenness and confession (where there has been wrong and unlove), or else as a loving challenge, as something that we ought to know about ourselves.[23]

It is a wholly submissive spirituality. One is prepared to submit to the loving need for group confession of wrong thoughts, attitudes and actions because Christ submitted himself for humanity in total surrender and brokenness. The aim is to create and then sustain a fellowship in which there is unclouded openness and trust between all the brothers and sisters who, together with Christ, share the status of total nothingness.

> Before we can enter the Highway, God must bend and break that stiff-necked self, so that Christ reigns in its stead. To be broken means to have no rights before God and man. It does not mean merely surrendering my rights to him, but rather recognizing that I haven't any, except to

[23] ibid., p. 24.

deserve hell. It means just being nothing and having nothing that I call my own, neither time, money, possessions, nor position. In order to break our wills to his, God brings us to the foot of the Cross and there shows us what real brokenness is.[24]

It is a spirituality which, in its moment-by-moment intensity, is very delicately poised between the riches of total trust and openness and the erosive possibilities of exclusiveness and super-spirituality. At its best, it is a vision of living under the daily impact of the cross of Christ which breeds deep care, love and supportiveness.

As a bishop in the Church of Uganda, Festo Kivengere stood squarely within the spirituality of the East African Revival. The testimony of his conversion experience encapsulates not only that particular emphasis, but provides a clear example of the place and importance of the cross which most evangelicals would own.

When I reached my room, I knelt by my bed, struggling for words to the One in whom I no longer believed. Finally I cried, 'God! If you happen to be there, as my friend says, I am miserable. If you can do anything for me, then please do it now. If I'm not too far gone . . . HELP!'

Then what happened in that room! Heaven opened, and in front of me was Jesus. He was there real and crucified for me. His broken body was hanging on the cross, and suddenly I knew that it was my badness that did this to the King of Life. It shook me. In tears, I thought I was going to hell. If he had said, 'Go!' I would not have complained. Somehow I thought that would be his duty, as all the wretchedness of my life came out.

But then I saw his eyes of infinite love which were looking into mine. Could it be he who was clearly saying, 'This is how much I love you, Festo!'

I shook my head, because I knew that couldn't be possible, and said, 'No, I am your enemy. I am rebellious. I

---

[24] ibid., p. 26.

have been hating your people. How can you love me like that?

Even today, I do not know the answer to that question. There is no reason in me for his love.

But that day I discovered myself clasped in the Father's arms. I was tattered and afraid, just like the younger son who went into the far country and then came to the end of himself. But why should the Father, who is holy, come running to hold me to his heart? I was dirty and desperate and had said and done much against him.

That love was wholly unexpected, but it filled my room, and I was convinced. He is the only one who loves the unlovable and embraces the unembraceable. In spite of what I was, I knew I was accepted, was a son of the Father, and that whatever Jesus did on the cross, it was for me.

Ever since that day, the cross has been central in my thinking, and the Lord Jesus my enabler for living near to it.[25]

Victory through the Cross of Christ

The classic view of the atonement which sees the cross of Christ as the place of victory over the powers of evil has not been absent in evangelicalism – Spurgeon made room for it in his preaching of the cross:

The cross was a battlefield to him, wherein he triumphed gloriously. He was fighting then with darkness; with the powers of darkness of which Satan is the head; with the darkness of human ignorance, depravity, and falsehood. The battle thus apparent at Golgotha has been raging ever since. Then was the conflict at its height ... All the powers of darkness in their dense battalions hurled themselves against the almighty Son of God. He bore their onset, endured the tremendous shock of their assault, and in the end, with a shout of victory, he led captivity captive. He by his power and Godhead turned midnight into day again,

[25] Festo Kivengere, *Revolutionary Love* (Eastbourne, Christian Literature Crusade 1985), pp. 16f.

and brought back to this world a ray of light which, blessed be God, shall never come to a close. Come to battle again, ye hosts of darkness, if ye dare! The cross has defeated you: the cross shall defeat you. Hallelujah![26]

Through the influence of charismatic renewal this emphasis on the victory of the cross has risen to greater prominence in many evangelical expositions of the atonement. The scope of Christ's victory has been broadened, in particular, by seeing the cross as the place of victory over both Satan and occult forces, and sickness and disease. Prayer for healing and deliverance now occupy a prominent place in many forms of evangelical spirituality in a way that was largely unknown before.

The victory of Christ over the devil, always a part of evangelicalism, is based on the conviction that 'The Son of God was revealed for this purpose, to destroy the works of the devil' (1 John 3:8). Charismatic renewal has emphasized, in addition, the victory of Christ over the world of evil spirits: 'He disarmed the rulers and authorities and made a public example of them, triumphing over them in it' (Colossians 2:15). Although there has been much disagreement on the precise nature of evil that underlies the ministry of deliverance across the whole range of charismatic evangelicalism, there is a widespread acceptance that evil spirits are presently active in society and individuals and that through the power of the cross they can be defeated. The re-emergence of widespread occult activity in Western societies has led many clergy and others, often reluctantly, to become involved in various forms of deliverance ministry.

As is common with new renewal movements, and also with such an area of ministry as this, it has provided a field day for sensationalists, and all kinds of extravagant and dangerous highjinks have been part of the 'deliverance scene'. Often this has revealed flights into non-biblical views of reality – a simplistic dualism, an over-developed view of personhood being attributed to evil forces, too little awareness of the destructive presence of evil within the powers and structures of this world, and an abolition of individual moral responsibility by regarding almost any compulsive pattern of sin as evidence of demon-possession. On the other hand, when part of a wise and discerning pastoral

[26] Spurgeon, op. cit., pp. 225f.

ministry, it can be an application of the victory of Christ over all that is evil in the whole created order, both spiritual and physical. It testifies to the glorious gospel truth that however pernicious the force of evil, however damaging and horrible its manifestation, it stands condemned and defeated by the power of Christ's self-sacrificing love.

The ministry of healing has most often been linked to the cross through the ministry of the Suffering Servant: 'Surely he has borne our infirmities and carried our diseases ... by his bruises we are healed' (Isaiah 53:4,5). The benefits of the passion include the physical as well as the spiritual. Like many others, David Watson, in his teaching, developed this into a broader understanding of salvation than had been normal in evangelicalism: 'The English word "salvation" is derived from the Latin *salvare*, "to save" and *salus*, "health" or "help". It means deliverance from danger or disease, and implies safety, health and prosperity.'[27] The victory of Christ is to do with wholeness, *shalom*; it operates in the realms of the communal and physical as well as the spiritual. Although any full experience of wholeness in all its dimensions must wait until the age to come, nevertheless it is possible to enter into varying degrees of that wholeness, including physical and emotional healing, in the present age. With this extended scope of the doctrine of the atonement there naturally followed a renewed emphasis on the gifts and ministry of healing, and the injunction of James influenced many evangelicals' approach to prayer and expectation of what God could do through the ministry of his children: 'Are any among you sick? They should call for the elders of the church and have them pray over them, anointing them with oil in the name of the Lord. The prayer of faith will save the sick' (James 5:14,15).

Where these two areas, deliverance and healing, have become part of evangelicalism, they have affected considerably the practice of prayer and corporate spirituality. There has been a much greater awareness of the place of the 'sacramental' in prayer – touch, the laying on of hands, the anointing with oil, the embrace – all have brought a new sacramentality and symbolism that had been largely absent in evangelical approaches to prayer. The

[27] David Watson, *Discipleship*, p. 101.

emphasis on healing, particularly inner and emotional healing, has deeply affected the corporate dimension of spirituality; it has fostered a strong commitment to openness and personal sharing, a relaxing of the 'stiff upper lip', a rejection of the lie that 'big boys don't cry', and an ability to show love more openly – all, in part, manifestations of the personal quality of the victory won by Christ on the cross.

The danger, of course, inherent in a strong emphasis on victory is the emergence of a triumphalistic spirituality. Evangelicalism has, from time to time, shown itself open to triumphalism, and that tendency has probably increased in the wake of certain kinds of charismatic enthusiasm. The 'prosperity gospel', which holds out the promise of material riches now as the result of faithfulness in God's service, is just one of the distortions of the gospel that has crept into certain circles via a myopic and wrongly focused view of the victory of Christ. Happily, for many, the increased emphasis on healing and personal relationships has led to an awareness of the vulnerability that lies deep within a Christlike understanding of victory – and thus a victorious gospel is not interpreted as one that proclaims slick results, looks for daily dramatic miracles, and then trumpets its shrill hallelujahs, but rather one that discovers that God's strength is victorious through our weakness, as it was in the cross of Jesus.

Family Groups within Spirituality

The cross dominates evangelical spirituality; it is the door into new life as well as the very atmosphere that permeates daily Christian experience. It clearly determines the family group to which evangelicalism belongs. Evangelicalism, through its focus on the cross, is a world-transforming spirituality.

It is a characteristic of most spiritualities that their central features are delineated by one or two cardinal doctrines whereas other important aspects of the faith influence them only peripherally. It is as a result of which doctrines most dominate that a spirituality finds itself in one of these main families: world-affirming (largely associated with creation and incarnation), world-transforming (focusing on the cross, the resurrection, or Pentecost), and world-denying (looking forward to the *eschaton*, or the blessings of heaven).

Evangelicalism is a world-transforming spirituality: everything must be changed, and this is accomplished through the cross of Christ, the great transaction between God and the world. Without the cross, the whole creation is lost in futility and impotence; through the cross, creation is redeemed, and the central ongoing feature of this redemption is seen as the personal transformation that delivers the individual from the darkness of sin and death into the glorious liberty of the children of God. The centrality of the cross ensures that evangelical spirituality, however often it may be side-tracked into world-denying attitudes (and we consider some examples of this in the next two chapters), will always veer back to its central powerful vision as 'world-transforming'.

Within the 'world-transforming' group of spiritualities it might seem more accurate to put evangelicalism in a sub-group named 'life-transforming' – because its emphasis is primarily on individual conversion rather than on the redemption of creation and humanity in its communal aspects. Such a reclassification, however, would fail to do justice to the evangelical understanding that world transformation is an important goal of salvation, but it is a goal that is accomplished largely through the conversion of individuals who make up the people of God and who then consciously seek to live out the prayer, 'Your kingdom come on earth as in heaven.' There are many examples of evangelical movements and individuals that have led to major social change as a result of their commitment to the transforming of the gospel. It is, moreover, an increasing feature of recent evangelical developments to emphasize the fundamental importance of the corporate and communal within salvation.

Spiritualities sometimes become world-denying when faced with opposition, oppression or persecution from other parts of the Church or society in general. When the experience of the present is so bad, the only hope is in the future to which one looks forward. Consequently, as slavery was such a degrading, oppressive and seemingly inescapable condition in this world, Negro spirituals express a spirituality that is often focused on the future release of heaven, as earthly experience is so irredeemably painful. Hope for the present is kept alive by the constant remembrance that 'this world is not my home, I'm just a-passing through.' The main world-denying forms of Western evangelicalism have been those influenced by an eschatology that sees the present world as one for which there is no hope apart from the imminent judgement of God, or that the rest of the Church is seen as so obdurate in its faithlessness that it is contaminating to associate with any outside of the select fellowship.

Evangelicalism has rarely been world-affirming, not having given pride of place to the doctrines of creation and incarnation. Indeed, evangelicals have tended to emphasize, more than many within the Western Augustinian tradition, the concept of original sin, thus giving more prominence to the fall tradition than to the original blessing of God's good creation. The fall, rather than creation, has a clear place within the evangelical tradition because it is the essential foundation in any evangelical doctrine of the cross. During the twentieth century, English evangelicals have maintained this cross-centred spirituality within a prevailing incarnation-centred theology which has been a marked feature of English Anglicanism since Charles Gore, in the Bampton Lectures of 1891, proclaimed the centrality of the incarnation in theology. Michael Ramsey, in the tradition of Charles Gore, considered the incarnation to have been central throughout the whole of Anglican history: 'It would be a bit of an oversimplification to say (but perhaps not too much of one) that in Anglican theology through the centuries the Incarnation has been a more central and prominent doctrine than that of the cross and redemption.'[28] History would suggest that Michael Ramsey was more than oversimplifying – it was a piece of special pleading. While there is much in the Anglican Reformation and Elizabethan settlement which provides a fertile seed-bed for an incarnationally-centred theology to germinate and flourish legitimately and healthily within Anglican soil, the place of redemption and atonement is explicitly central within the Articles of Religion, the Book of Common Prayer, and the Homilies which expound the faith of the reformed Church of England. One of the reasons for the conflicts between evangelicals and others within the Church of England is the existence of these two theological traditions, especially when both sides have, at times, seemed determined to disprove the validity and legitimacy

---

[28] Michael Ramsey, *The Anglican Spirit* (London, SPCK 1991), pp. 21f.

of the other, rather than working at a spirituality whose richness is to make room for both within the totality of its understanding of the Christian faith.

The resurrection, ascension and Pentecost also stand along-side the cross as those doctrines which, when central, create a world-transforming spirituality. They have rarely been prominent features alongside the cross within evangelicalism,[29] thus delineating even more precisely the exact nature of its world-transforming agenda. Pentecost, in so many traditions the minor player, has been given a new and leading role within many sections of evangelicalism during this century through Pentecos-talism and the growth of charismatic emphases. In essence, this injection into evangelicalism promises to make it more world-affirming, more strongly committed to transformation, more orientated towards mission and the world, especially when it moves beyond the inward-looking pietism which has infected some groups in the initial stages.

It is in the Eastern tradition that we see the centrality of the resurrection and the ascension, which creates a world-trans-forming character very different from that within evangelical spirituality. There we see a faith which transforms the poverty of earthly existence by establishing within it the transforming glory of the risen, ascended and glorified Lord. The world is transformed by experiencing within its own context the glory of the worship of heaven. It is thus a world-transforming spiritu-ality that, in practice, seems far removed from evangelicalism, having as it does a strong liturgical and corporate emphasis as a central mark of its transforming character. But though it seems different in feel, because of its essential type within the family of Christian spiritualities, it is a near relative of evangelical spirituality such that when an evangelical believer discovers the desire for the liturgical and the corporate, the spirituality of Eastern Orthodoxy is often a more natural environment than many emphases within Western Catholicism.

---

[29] The resurrection is always part of the evangelical understanding of the cross as the Jesus who died is proclaimed as the living Saviour. One of the reasons (the other being the fear of idolatry) why evangelicals have tended to prefer a cross to a crucifix as a symbol of the death of Christ is because the empty cross symbolizes the atonement viewed from a resurrection perspective.

5

THE PURSUIT OF HOLINESS

While we do his good will,
He abides with us still,
And with all who will trust and obey.

Holiness, for the evangelical, is not primarily a religious concept, it is a moral category. It is to do with daily living, and applying biblical standards of morality and behaviour in personal, corporate and national life. It is not particularly to do with the extent of a person's commitment to the practice of prayer, or how deeply they have grown in the life of prayer. Naturally these are both part of any understanding of holiness, as one's outer life and active behaviour are vitally connected with the character and quality of one's prayer life – but holiness is not understood predominantly in relation to a person's religious observances. Even less, within evangelical circles, is holiness seen as having much, if anything, to do with holy moments, holy places, holy buildings, special categories of holy people (e.g., priests, nuns, and monks). It is a much broader concept. It will at times include these more specifically religious categories but, in essence, it is to do with the total life of obedience before God.

Walking with the Lord

This holiness of life is focused in the daily living relationship with Christ. 'To walk with the Lord' is the time-honoured evangelical way of speaking about holiness. As the focus of that daily walk one has one's eyes fixed on Christ, 'looking unto Jesus', following the injunction to holiness of living in Hebrews 12:1,2 – '. . . let us also lay aside every weight and the sin that clings so closely, and let us run with perseverance the race that is set before us, looking to Jesus the pioneer and perfecter of our faith . . .' This walk in holiness that is focused on Christ is the theme of the popular evangelical hymn, written in 1912 by Katie Wilkinson (1859–1928):

> May the mind of Christ my Saviour
> Live in me from day to day,
> By his love and power controlling
> All I do and say.

Holiness is dependent on the closest of unions between Christ and the individual. The mind, the power and the love of Christ are important simply because the corresponding attributes in us are perilously weakened by our fallen condition. Our mind is darkened so that we cannot see clearly what is right, our power to obey God is markedly feeble and inconsistent, and our love is too fickle and self-centred to sustain a Christlike lifestyle. The holiness which results from this close daily relationship with Christ, is often characteristically portrayed as a well-poised life:

> May the peace of God my Father
> Rule my life in everything,
> That I may be calm to comfort
> Sick and sorrowing.

But it is clear that such peace and contentment is immediately seen within a missionary context. It is of the essence of evangelicalism to see all personal growth and blessing as providing first and foremost greater freedom and opportunity to be actively involved in the service of God. It is therefore a holiness which, for all its poise and equanimity, must be approached with zest and vigour:

> May I run the race before me,
> Strong and brave to face the foe,
> Looking only unto Jesus
> As I onward go.

Although this hymn bears witness to that combination of rest and vigorous activity which portrays evangelicalism at its active best, it most adequately expresses the gentler qualities of holiness. This emphasis is more noticeable in hymnody than in the daily, more activity-centred experience of many evangelicals – and for two reasons. Firstly, there is a quietist thread running through the movement, one which, understandably, is far more readily expressed by the poets (hymn-writers) of the movement than by many of its leaders who are ever urging others into active service. Secondly, as we have noticed already, a large proportion of the evangelical hymn-writers have been women and, certainly in Victorian and Edwardian times, the themes of submission and passive obedience would have been accepted virtues for a woman, particularly a respectable middle- or upper-class evangelical one! On the other hand, hymns like 'Soldiers of Christ arise' (Charles Wesley 1707–88) and 'Stand up, stand up for Jesus' (George Duffield 1818–88) are quite clearly masculine compositions (the second being written specifically to be sung at a men's meeting) which expresses the active thrust of most evangelical approaches to holiness.

'Take my life . . .'

The most celebrated evangelical hymn on the theme of holiness is, without doubt, 'Take my life, and let it be consecrated, Lord, to thee', composed by the movement's most famous female hymn-writer, Frances Ridley Havergal (1836–79). Here, consecration, being set aside in holiness for the service of the Lord, is dominated by the longing that the whole of one's being should be at the free disposal of Christ. When life is lived under the lordship and kingship of Christ daily living becomes an act of worship.[1]

> Take my life, and let it be
> Consecrated, Lord, to thee;

[1] As one of evangelicalism's favourite female hymn-writers, Frances Ridley Havergal recognized the difference that her sex (and we would add, her culture!), made to her compositions. *Master* was her favourite title for Jesus because it 'implies rule and submission which is what love craves'. She also observed, 'Men may feel differently, but a true woman's submission is inseparable from deep love.'

> Take my moments and my days,
> Let them flow in ceaseless praise.

Although consecration and holiness are seen in the context of worship, that worship is not thought of in terms of religious observance, holy things and special places. Worship, consecration and holiness are the stuff of everyday Christian living, seen as a personal and daily submission to Christ. The place of sacred worship is not so much a special building; it is the interior meeting place between Christ and the individual:

> Take my will, and make it thine;
> It shall be no longer mine.
> Take my heart, it is thine own;
> It shall be thy royal throne.

The occasion of the writing of this hymn sets holiness firmly within the context of service for Christ, and what, for many, is the supreme manifestation of such service – leading others to a living relationship with God. She explains the circumstances of what happened during a five-day visit to friends at Areley House in Worcestershire in February 1874:

> There were ten persons in the house, some unconverted and long prayed for, some converted but not rejoicing Christians. He gave me the prayer, 'Lord, give me all in this house!' and he just *did*! Before I left the house everyone had got a blessing. The last night of my visit, after I had retired, the governess asked me to go to the two daughters. They were crying, etc; then and there both of them trusted and rejoiced; it was nearly midnight. I was too happy to sleep, and spent most of the night in praise and renewal of my own consecration; and these little couplets formed themselves, and chimed in my heart one after another, till they finished with, 'Ever, ONLY, ALL for thee!'

For Frances Ridley Havergal such a surrender to Christ on the part of all in the household would be seen, in part, as a consequence of her own consecration. Even more significantly, she would regard it as a reason for ever deeper consecration to the service of the Lord who had deigned to use her in such a fashion. The final two couplets express the extravagance and joyful abandonment evident in such surrender to holiness:

> Take my love; my Lord, I pour
> At thy feet its treasure store.
> Take myself, and I will be
> Ever, only, all for thee.

Subsequently, Miss Havergal wrote her own commentary on this hymn in *Kept for the Master's Use*. In that exposition, she changes the word, *Take*, which begins each couplet, to *Keep* (it was originally written in couplets, not in the four-line verses as we know it). The reason for this change is to show that 'consecration is not so much a step as a course; not so much an act as a position to which a course of action inseparably belongs . . . We do not want to go on taking a first step over and over again. What we want now is to be maintained in that position and fulfil that course.'

To turn from the female hymn-writers and poets of the movement to a person more typical of its masculine leadership in a former age, Bishop Ryle gives a helpful summary of an evangelical approach to holiness in the first chapter of *Practical Religion*.

> Genuine Scriptural holiness will make a man do his duty at home and by the fireside, and adorn his doctrine in the little trials of daily life. It will exhibit itself in passive graces as well as in active. It will make a man humble, kind, gentle, unselfish, good-tempered, considerate for others, loving, meek, and forgiving. It will not constrain him to go out of the world, and shut himself up in a cave like a hermit. But it will make him do his duty in that state to which God has called him, on Christian principles, and after the pattern of Christ.[2]

[2] J. C. Ryle, *Practical Religion* (reprinted 1959 by James Clarke, London), p. 9. As I mention later in this chapter, there have been some very significant differences of emphasis about how holiness becomes a reality in a Christian's life. J. C. Ryle stands in the Calvinist and Puritan tradition within evangelicalism and his writings were written as a deliberate attempt to refute what some other evangelicals were teaching. However, much of his exposition of *holiness*, as with this extract, is common ground among evangelicals.

It is necessary to place this practical emphasis alongside the commitment to holiness within the hymns of evangelical piety. Such hymns can encourage, and in some instances have encouraged, the idea that holiness is to do solely with the inner relationship between the individual and Christ. 'Take my life' clearly refers to some far-reaching practical implications of consecration, but its poetic cast, and the variety of soft mellifluous tunes to which it is usually sung, together with the golden rays of the setting sun falling gently on the congregation when this hymn is sung at the end of an evening service, can suggest warmth and intensity of devotion, rather than the tough, challenging demands of holiness in daily life!

Holiness in Contention

Very little further progress can be made in discussing evangelical understandings of holiness without facing its central issue: To what extent is holiness produced by our efforts, or the work of God within us? Time and again, evangelical teaching on holiness has sought to resolve the essential mystery at the heart of Paul's teaching on the subject: 'Work out your own salvation with fear and trembling; for it is God who is at work in you, enabling you both to will and to work for his good pleasure' (Philippians 2:12,13).

Many evangelicals have been content with a straightforward exposition of the teaching of these verses, like this outline by Oswald Sanders of the Overseas Missionary Fellowship, one of evangelicalism's leading interdenominational missionary societies, and as such, a major influence on popular spirituality:

> It is not always easy to discern where God's part in the work of sanctification ends and where man's begins. There is something which God alone can do, and something which man alone can do . . . Christian character does not just happen. We have a contribution to make to our own sanctification . . . We have at our disposal the limitless resources of God. These have been placed to our credit in the bank of heaven. That is God's part. But we must draw and present the cheques.[3]

[3] J. Oswald Sanders, *The Best that I Can Be* (London, Overseas Missionary Fellowship 1988), pp. 64f.

Many have been unsatisfied by what they see as a lack of precision in such definitions, and on numerous occasions, more particular positions have been adopted. Some have desired a more probing understanding, while others have re-emphasized some forgotten evangelical teaching from the past. Often people have felt that there are deeper spiritual resources to be discovered, or new and vivid experiences have come to individuals and groups of Christians which require fresh explanations; yet others have become aware of new insights in contemporary society which have altered the way Christians approach the question of holiness and which need to be evaluated in the light of the scriptures. All of these, and more, have led to different ways of describing the relationship between the work of God and human effort within the process of sanctification.

It will be necessary to look at several of these because they have had such an impact on the development of evangelical spirituality, as well as leading to some of the sharpest disagreements. However, it is possible to separate out those areas of substantial agreement within evangelicalism that, together, make up the generally agreed fundamentals about holiness (though even here there will be some who will want to reserve judgement on one or two of the emphases I choose, or the way in which I happen to describe them here!). Notwithstanding, it is necessary to make the attempt, because any coherent understanding of evangelical spirituality depends on a grasp of the central dynamics of an evangelical spiritual theology of holiness.

(1) True human happiness is found in a life of holiness that is rooted in the very nature of God himself. Christians are to be holy because God is holy (1 Peter 1:15,16). As God is set apart from all that is evil and corrupting so we, his children, are to exhibit a similar apartness from all that is morally defiling: we must reflect the family likeness. Thus, holiness is not a negative concept but, essentially, one that is positive, progressive and visionary, setting goals that give meaning and direction to life. The desire for holiness evokes the ambition to reflect the very nature, wholeness and wholesomeness of God himself. It is, therefore, not to do with obeying a list of rules and regulations but about the totality of a person's ability to live to the full the human life that God intends for all who are made in his image. Charles Simeon

catches well the tone of holiness as a life that reflects the nature of God:

> There will be in him more solidity, more consistency. His principles will be more and more commended to all around him by their efficacy to beautify his soul and to adorn his life. In a word, he will be renewed, not in his mind only, but in the spirit of his mind, and will become an epistle of Christ 'known and read of all men', an epistle not written by any human hand, but by 'the Spirit of the living God'. He will be in himself (and will constrain all who know him to acknowledge that he is) what the scriptures emphatically call, 'a man of God'.[4]

Holiness is not a glamorous pursuit reaping quick rewards. Simeon's word, *solidity*, conveys the sense of serious purpose that lies at the heart of a desire for holiness. It is at variance with the more ephemeral trappings sometimes found amongst evangelicals. It reminds us that, behind the thrill, the warmth, the endeavour and the excitement, there is that solid, though still deeply joyful, commitment to reflect the holiness of God in the ordinary behaviour of our everyday life – both when we are visible to our fellow human beings, and when we are seen by God alone.

As William Law's book reminds us, we are confronted with *A Serious Call to a Devout and Holy Life* – but not to a dull, dreary, withering existence.

> The more we discover God in everything, the more we seek him in every place, the more we look up to him in all our actions, the more we conform to his will, the more we act according to his wisdom and imitate his goodness, so much the more we enjoy God. Then we share in the divine nature and heighten and increase all that is happy and comfortable in human life.[5]

---

[4] From Simeon's address, 'The Spirit's Work in Believers' reprinted in *Let Wisdom Judge*, pp. 147f.

[5] From chapter 11, *A Serious Call to a Devout and Holy Life*, originally published in 1729, was a great influence on John Wesley, as it was on many of Law's other contemporaries. It has become one of the classics of a quintessentially English Protestant spirituality. The quotation is from the edition of Halcyon Backhouse (London, Hodder and Stoughton 1987), p. 92.

The holiness of God is to do with true happiness; it is not a life of negative privation. 'The chief end of man is to glorify God and to enjoy him forever', asserts the opening sentence of the Westminster Confession of Faith. Jesus was not Swinburne's 'pale Galilean' but the one who exhorted us to discover happiness in the pursuit of holiness, to discover the joys and life-enhancing possibilities of meekness, righteousness, mercy and purity (Matthew 5:1–10). It is important to establish the centrality of the joy of holiness in view of the common misconception that evangelical views of holiness lead to a life hedged around with gloomy prohibitions. This was, of course, characteristic of the famous portrayals of evangelicals in the Victorian novel. George Elliot paints the type so well – and with more subtlety and humour than many:

> Evangelicalism was no longer a nuisance existing merely in by-corners, which any well-clad person could avoid; it was invading the drawing rooms, mingling itself with the comfortable fumes of port-wine and brandy, threatening to deaden with its murky breath all the splendour of the ostrich feathers.[6]

Such a picture would not be difficult to discover in the real-life history of evangelicalism. It did become one of the dominant influences in Victorian middle-class culture, and the tendency to enjoy being morally superior about one's supposed holiness, rather than enjoying the pursuit and the fruits of holiness itself, is a recurring temptation in evangelicalism – and elsewhere.

The pursuit of holiness seems a veritable minefield waiting to defeat even the most alert. For anyone who is serious and in earnest about holiness, the danger is that the very seriousness of the endeavour itself leads to a loss of joy and lightness of spirit, which lies at the heart of the maturing and humanizing work of sanctification. Charles Simeon, who carried the heavy burden of the evangelical cause for so long, typifies the problem of serious intent turning into a rather forbidding, humourless

---

[6] From 'Janet's Repentance' in *Scenes of Clerical Life* (1858, republished London 1973) p. 263. In 'Janet's Repentance', the story of the influence on individuals and the community of an evangelical curate, the general portrayal of evangelicalism is a positive one.

and sombre seriousness. Having quoted him to his credit, it is only fair to use him to show up the warts of his tradition also!

> The impression that one gets is that he knew he ought, as a Christian, to be cheerful. He realized 'what a gloomy and repellent effect it would have were I a man who dared not smile or laugh'. 'I strive always to be cheerful, and to make religion attractive to the eye of those with whom, in the situation in which God has placed me, I am called into contact. To the ungodly I am a scarecrow, I know, for they avoid the sight of me; but to other young men I do not find it so.'[7]

This is not significantly different in style from what we can observe in many others who are serious about religion, in whatever tradition, though evangelicalism seems to have been one of the major contributors to this tendency within the British Isles!

(2) Holiness is based on the free gift of justification by faith, and cannot be earned by works of merit. This is the truth for which evangelicals have always contended vigorously. A person is not saved through works of the law but by God's grace through faith in the finished work of Christ's death and resurrection. The life of holiness to which we are called by God is founded on this work of grace within the individual. It is not holiness that wins us acceptance with God, but his acceptance of us which is the basis for growth in holiness. We are accepted as holy by the Father because we have been clothed with Christ's righteousness. We begin the pursuit of holiness not because we see it as something to attain in order to make us acceptable to God, but because we have been forgiven and set free by the amazing grace and generosity of God.

It is this conviction that has sometimes led to views of cheap grace and to antinomianism – the very thought of which so offended St Paul: 'Should we continue in sin in order that grace may abound? By no means!' (Romans 6:1,2). Paul's answer is the only one to give. The antinomian suggestion is one that is

[7] Hugh Evan Hopkins, *Charles Simeon of Cambridge* (London, Hodder and Stoughton 1977), p. 161.

so unworthy that it must not be dignified by lengthy consideration. The pursuit of holiness is a natural and instinctive way of expressing gratitude to God for his astounding generosity in forgiveness and new life. It is morally unimaginable (even if logically conceivable in the abstract), that this new resurrection-life that began with the forgiveness of sin – at the cost of the death of Christ – should be worked out in careless sinning.

We do, of course, live with the awareness that sin still lurks menacingly within each one of us; and it is still one of the most significant contributions we bring to the personal processes of growth. Indeed, the more we grow in holiness, the more we recognize the subtle power of the tendency to sin and disobedience that is always ready to despoil the fruits of Christlike living. Nevertheless the pursuit of holiness is a way of freedom, a journey in which we can expect to discover the true value of the liberation that is now ours in Christ. No longer is the Christian burdened by the guilt of past sin, or paralysed by the inevitability of failure. Every day is full of renewed opportunities to live in the freedom and holiness of Christ.

(3) Holiness is grounded in our identification with Christ who is the source and motivation for our growth and maturity. St Paul speaks of our new life in Christ in terms of being baptized into Christ's death in order to be raised with him in the new resurrection life (Romans 6). It is this identification with Christ that provides the framework for holy living. As we have died to sin, it must be our concern to ensure that sin no longer exercises dominion over us (v.12). Our identification with Christ gives the clearest motivation for holiness. As those who are 'in Christ', we are to live towards God the Father as Christ lived in loving obedience before him.

As we are united with Christ, the Christian's basic motivation is naturally towards holiness. Again, there is no hint in this vision of holiness of the negative associations that so often surround the idea. Essentially, we are called to say 'Yes' to what, deep down, we most want to be 'in Christ', rather than saying 'No' to what we would rather do. Our deepest desire should be to love God, to do what he wants, to honour him, to serve him, and to work out in practice what is present within, as a result of the new person we are in Christ.

The Chinese Christian, Watchman Nee, describes identification with Christ in a way that has been an eye-opener for many:

> God has done the work in Christ and not in us as individuals. The all-inclusive death and the all-inclusive resurrection of God's Son were accomplished fully and finally apart from us in the first place. It is the history of *Christ* which is to become the experience of the Christian, and we have no spiritual experience apart from him . . . In the scriptures we find that no Christian experience exists *as such*. What God has done in his gracious purpose is to include us in Christ.[8]

At the very heart of an evangelical spiritual theology is the question: 'Am I responding to the motivation towards Christlikeness and holiness that is fundamentally part of who I am in Christ?' If I am 'in Christ' there should inevitably be real evidence of holiness. If there is no such evidence, the question follows: 'Am I truly in Christ?' Consequently, though some evangelicals have been worried by the use of Hebrews 12:14, 'Pursue . . . holiness without which no one will see the Lord' (because they have, wrongly, imagined it to imply salvation by works), most recognize the ontological inseparability of holiness and incorporation into Christ.

(4) Holiness delights in the law of God as the way of love and freedom: it rejects legalism and casuistry as the way of fear and bondage. Because we are motivated towards holiness we will love the law of God as fulfilled and interpreted by Christ. We should so want to be holy that we welcome God's law, not as some nit-picking legalism, but because by it, we are guided into a clearer understanding of holiness and Christlikeness. Because children of God know the Holy Father to be all-loving, there is no dichotomy between lawgiving and unconditional love. God's children understand that the law is perfect and given to help them attain the true humanity in Christ to which they are called. Out of deep gratitude and love, they will seek to please the

[8] Watchman Nee, *The Normal Christian Life*, pp. 53f.

Father by joyful and willing obedience. 'If you love me, you will keep my commandments' (John 14:15).

We accept that God expresses his holiness, and provides guidelines to enable us to reflect that holiness, in the form of law, which is holy, just and good (Romans 7:12). We recognize the elucidation of this law of God throughout the scriptures in the Ten Commandments, the teachings of the prophets, the apostles and Christ himself. As did St Paul, we must recognize the continuing place of God's law throughout our Christian pilgrimage: 'I am not free from God's law but am under Christ's law' (1 Corinthians 9:21). We rejoice that we are free from the curse of the law and bondage to its demands which we know can never be satisfied by human effort. But we rejoice in the freedom of being justified and living as free men and women under the law of Christ as the standard to follow in seeking to live out the holiness of life into which we have entered by the free gift of God.

(5) Holiness involves a life-long process of transformation. Sanctification (*hagiasmos*) describes the process involved in becoming ever more holy, whole, and mature in Christ. It begins with the initial setting apart by God of each believer to be consecrated to him: 'You were washed, you were sanctified, you were justified in the name of the Lord Jesus Christ and in the Spirit of our God' (1 Corinthians 6:11). Sanctification continues as we seek more and more to become, in reality, the kind of people we have been made in Christ. 'For this is the will of God, your sanctification . . .' (1 Thessalonians 4:3). Our responsibility is one of daily commitment to live lives that exhibit the holiness and righteousness of God: 'I appeal to you therefore, brothers and sisters, by the mercies of God, to present your bodies as a living sacrifice, holy and acceptable to God, which is your spiritual worship. Do not be conformed to this world, but be transformed by the renewing of your minds . . .' (Romans 12:1,2). This transformation must become the longing of our prayers for ourselves and for others: 'May the God of peace sanctify you entirely; and may your spirit and soul and body be kept sound and blameless at the coming of our Lord Jesus Christ. The one who calls you is faithful, and he will do this' (1 Thessalonians 5:23,24). There are no short cuts to holiness, no

secrets that suddenly produce a Christlike character. Growth, maturing, the formation of Christlike habits, the conscious commitment to ongoing change – all these are fundamental in a realistic and biblical understanding of holiness. Though many, at different times, and in different ways, may go through crisis moments which greatly encourage this process of sanctification (maybe even giving a glimpse of the end of the journey), holiness always remains a process in which there is more to discover as long as we remain in this life.

This process of growth in holiness was something to which St Paul was energetically committed, for others, as for himself. He described the Galatian Christians as 'my little children, for whom I am again in the pain of childbirth until Christ is formed in you' (Galatians 4:19). As Christians, we are called to be committed to our brothers and sisters in their growth in holiness – not in some fault-finding, holier-than-thou attitude, but out of a genuine concern for their deepest happiness, welfare and effectiveness. Consequently we will keep no score of wrongs nor take pleasure in the sins of others (1 Corinthians 13:6): rather we will seek to encourage one another and 'see how each of us may best arouse others to love and active goodness' (Hebrews 10:24 REB).

But in our care for others we must never neglect our own need to grow in holiness. We must exert vigorous effort on our own behalf if the process of transformation is not to grind to a halt, and maybe even go into reverse. St Paul counsels us to be like athletes who exercise self-control in everything, and expresses his own commitment to the pursuit of holiness with a most unequivocal expression: 'So I do not run aimlessly, nor do I box as though beating the air; but I punish my body and enslave it, so that after proclaiming to others I myself should not be disqualified' (1 Corinthians 9:26,27).[9] In part, we show our diligence in the pursuit of holiness by employing all the

---

[9] We would be unjustified in taking this vigorous expression of St Paul as an encouragement to various kinds of ascetic self-flagellation. Paul is retaining the metaphor of boxing which he has been using. 'The body is not evil, but it must be made to serve the right master, not the wrong one. This moreover is not something that may be done once without necessity of repetition.' C. K. Barrett, *A Commentary on the First Epistle to the Corinthians* (London, A. & C. Black, second edition 1971), p. 218.

means of grace which God has given. On this point, also, Bishop Ryle is in his usual emphatic mood:

> When I speak of 'means', I have in view Bible-reading, private prayer, regular attendance on public worship, regular hearing of God's Word, and regular reception of the Lord's Supper. I lay it down as a simple matter of fact, that no one who is careless about such things must ever expect to make much progress in sanctification. I can find no record of any eminent saint who ever neglected them. They are appointed channels through which the Holy Spirit conveys fresh supplies of grace to the soul, and strengthens the work which he has begun in the inward man. Let men call this legal doctrine if they please, but I will never shrink from declaring my belief that there are no 'spiritual gains without pains'.[10]

(6) Holiness is the fruit of the work of the Holy Spirit within the life of an obedient and responsive believer. Paul speaks of all Christians being transformed into the likeness of Christ 'from one degree of glory to another; for this comes from the Lord, the Spirit' (2 Corinthians 3:18). Thus, for all the human effort that goes into our sanctification, at its most profound, holiness is a supernatural work of God within. This realization creates in us an openness to the energizing work of the Spirit, for we know that, of ourselves, we cannot attain the image of Christ. We acknowledge that the endless turning over of new leaves, the annually (or more frequently) renewed resolutions, and the genuine longings to be so much better in the way we live, produce a very poor crop. But, as we seek to live in obedience to God, so the Holy Spirit is making something infinitely better of us than we could achieve ourselves – the fruit of which is 'love, joy, peace, patience, kindness, generosity, faithfulness, gentleness, and self-control' (Galatians 5:22,23). In this process the Holy Spirit is our counsellor and it is he who determines the appropriate steps in holiness to be taken at each stage of the journey. This 'process cannot be rushed by overloading the conscience . . . God will proceed at a rate and follow a course

---

[10] J. C. Ryle, *Holiness* (James Clarke 1952), p. 21.

which are ideally suited to the individual, raising successive issues over the years . . . He seldom shows us all of our needs at once; we would be overwhelmed at the sight.'[11] A concern to preserve the direct role of the Spirit in the process of sanctification has been one of the reasons for evangelical hesitancy over the place of spiritual direction; nothing must compromise the freedom of the Spirit to be the Director who needs no intermediaries. More recently, the greater openness within evangelicalism to learn from other traditions has led many to see the value of sensitive and discerning human agency within this directing work of the Spirit.

At the heart of the Spirit's work is the renewing of our minds (Romans 12:2) to conform our ways of thinking and judging to the desires and perspectives of God. Evidence of this maturing and sanctifying work of the Spirit is seen in the seemingly natural, instinctive godliness of judgement, in the way of perceiving and reacting which takes on an increasingly Christlike quality in the lives of Christians who are submitting their minds to God. John Newton gives us an instance of such maturity in holiness:

> Prudence is a word much abused; but there is a heavenly wisdom, which the Lord has promised to give to those who humbly wait upon him for it. It does not consist in forming a bundle of rules and maxims, but in a spiritual taste and discernment, derived from an experimental knowledge of the truth, and of the heart of man, as described in the word of God.[12]

In our co-operation with the work of the Spirit within, Paul warns, 'Do not grieve the Holy Spirit of God' (Ephesians 4:30). The context makes plain that we do this when we persist in unwholesome living. On the positive side, Paul exhorts us to be filled with the Spirit (Ephesians 5:18). We are called daily to make ourselves available for the free working of God's Spirit: we are to give that space and permission for him to influence us, call us, lead us, encourage us, and remould us. In readiness

---

[11] Richard Lovelace, *Dynamics of Spiritual Life* (Exeter, Paternoster Press 1979) p. 111.

[12] John Newton, *Cardiphonia* (Morgan and Scott 1911), pp. 197f.

for this we must acknowledge that there are other influences which must be excluded. In the Ephesian context Paul was thinking of the effects of excessive alcohol – there are clearly many other influences that we can allow to be at work within us instead of looking for the continual infilling of the Holy Spirit.

This injunction to be filled with the Spirit is also seen by Paul in the context of worship – 'as you sing psalms and hymns and spiritual songs among yourselves, singing and making melody to the Lord in your hearts, giving thanks to God the Father at all times and for everything in the name of our Lord Jesus Christ' (Ephesians 5:19,20). Worship is important in our growth in holiness because it is the environment in which the individual and the community of faith are most conscious of the free presence of God by his Spirit: the presence of the Spirit leads us into worship and is also evoked afresh within the life of the community by that worship.

(7) Holiness is the basis for Christian effectiveness. Consecration and holiness are the foundation for serving God (2 Timothy 2:21). Comprehending the will of God is a consequence of holiness of life (Romans 12:1,2), and effective prayer depends on a similar commitment. When we pray we are to lift up *holy* hands (1 Timothy 2:8). If we are not approaching God in prayer from the background of holy living then we court the stern rebuke issued by Isaiah: 'When you stretch out your hands, I will hide my eyes from you; even though you make many prayers, I will not listen; your hands are full of blood' (Isaiah 1:15).

Effectiveness in Christ's service is related to holiness of life. While it is common throughout the Church to hold that the sacraments are not called into question by the unworthiness of the minister, it is the recurring evidence of evangelical ministers and their congregations that effectiveness for God in ministry presupposes holiness. Robert Murray McCheyne spoke for many when he wrote:

> In great measure, according to the purity and perfections of the instrument, will be the success. It is not great talents God blesses so much as great likeness to Jesus. A holy minister is an awful weapon in the hands of God . . . How

much more useful might we be, if we were only more free from pride, self-conceit, personal vanity, or some secret sin that a heart knows.[13]

Holiness influences not only the effectiveness of Christian service but also our sense of contentment. Once a person has become a new creation in Christ, there is nothing more uncomfortable than returning to ways of living that are incompatible with union with Christ. There is a distinct lack of ease at the heart of such double-mindedness. The presence of God's Spirit becomes not only disturbing (as is often the case) but accusing (which is not God's intention for the ministry of the Spirit in the believers). To persist in a relationship with God that brings contentment and well-being there must be a commitment to holiness, because that is the commitment of God who is at work in us. Turning again to some words of Bishop Ryle –

> We are sadly apt to forget that there is a close connection between sin and sorrow, holiness and happiness, sanctification and consolation. God has so wisely ordered it, that our well-being and our well-doing are linked together. He has mercifully provided that even in this world it shall be man's interest to be holy . . . A believer may as soon expect to feel the sun's rays upon a dark and cloudy day, as to feel strong consolation in Christ while he does not follow him fully . . . Oh, for our own sakes, if there were no other reason, let us strive to be holy! He that follows Jesus more fully will always follow him more comfortably.[14]

(8) Holiness is costly. In his earthly ministry large crowds were following Jesus: there was a deep attraction to him and his call to discipleship, yet he was concerned that they would make commitments and promises that failed to count the cost. So that they would be under no illusions, he painted the picture very starkly, 'Whoever comes to me and does not hate father and mother, wife and children, brothers and sisters, yes and even

[13] From letters written to two ministers in 1840 and recorded in Andew Bonar, *Memoir and Remains of the Rev R. M. McCheyne* (Edinburgh 1844), pp. 282, 288.

[14] *Holiness*, p. 43.

life itself, cannot be my disciple. Whoever does not carry the cross and follow me cannot be my disciple . . . None of you can become my disciple if you do not give up all of your possessions' (Luke 14:26–33). Expressed in the idiom of his day, Jesus is calling for a love and loyalty which is exclusive, which makes love for God a priority even over one's dearest relatives. There is no escaping the radical nature of the call to discipleship – the cost of holiness, being set apart for God, is crystal clear.

Paul found that Demas was not able to face the cost of this calling – 'Demas, in love with this present world, has deserted me' (2 Timothy 4:10). He had previously been counted among Paul's fellow workers (Colossians 4:14; Philemon 24). He had found the cost of being thus set apart too great. Bishop Ryle expected that all who called others to Christian discipleship should tell the whole truth – including the cost (an injunction which some evangelists, in their enthusiasm for 'converts' have foolishly, and short-sightedly, omitted to do):

> Work hard if you will, and have the opportunity for the souls of others. Press them to consider their ways. Compel them with holy violence to come in, to lay down their arms, and to yield themselves to God. Offer them salvation, ready, free, full, immediate salvation. Press Christ and all his benefits on their acceptance. But in all your work tell the truth. Be ashamed to use the vulgar art of a recruiting serjeant. Do not speak only of the uniform, the pay and the glory; speak also of the enemies, the battle, the armour, the watching, the marching, the drill. Do not present only one side of Christianity. Do not keep back 'the cross' of self-denial that must be carried, when you speak of the cross on which Christ died for our redemption. Explain fully what Christianity entails. Entreat men to repent and come to Christ; but bid them at the same time to 'count the cost'.[15]

(9) Holiness is central to God's eternal purpose for the whole of humanity and is the future goal of all the redeemed community. To be committed to growth in holiness is to be in touch and in

[15] ibid., p. 77.

harmony with the very heart of God's eternal purposes: 'He chose us in Christ before the foundation of the world to be holy and blameless before him in love' (Ephesians 1:4). To choose anything other than holiness as one's goal in life is to opt for a way of living that is out of tune with the basic, indwelling, God-given motivation for human growth and development. The reason Christ gave his life for the sake of the Church was 'to make her holy by cleansing her with the washing of water by the word, so as to present the church to himself in splendour, without a spot or wrinkle or anything of the kind – yes, so that she may be holy and without blemish' (Ephesians 5:26,27). The completion of that process towards holiness which begins with repentance and faith in Christ is through the resurrection of the body as the community of believers enters into the fullness of God's presence – we shall then stand justified, sanctified and free in the very presence of God in all his holiness.

The need to be ready to enter into the conscious awareness of the holiness of God in heaven was expressed much more forcefully in a former age than it is today – but it remains part of evangelical spirituality:

> I appeal solemnly to everyone who reads these pages, How shall we ever be at home and happy in heaven, if we die unholy? Death works no change. The grave makes no alteration. Each will rise again with the same character in which he breathed his last. Where will our place be if we are strangers to holiness now?[16]

Does the Way of Holiness Lead through Struggle and Conflict?

There are many, including myself, who would want to add a tenth point in order to complete the evangelical view of holiness – one that points to the ongoing struggle and conflict inevitably involved in the pursuit of holiness. But such a section must stand somewhat on its own as it represents the area of great debate and division within evangelical spiritual theology. I include it at this point because I believe the majority of evangelicals would want to affirm it to some degree or other. I will let Ryle take up the issue in his normal picturesque style:

[16] ibid., p. 44.

The principal fight of the Christian is with the world, the
flesh, and the devil. These are his never dying foes. These
are the chief enemies against whom he must wage war.
Unless he gets the victory over these three, all other victor-
ies are useless and vain. If he had a nature like an angel,
and were not a fallen creature, the warfare would not be
so essential. But with a corrupt heart, a busy devil, and an
ensnaring world, he must either 'fight' or be lost.[17]

In our struggle to live holy lives we are encouraged by the
struggle inherent in Jesus' earthly life: 'Consider him who
endured such hostility against himself from sinners, so that you
may not grow weary or lose heart. In your struggle against sin
you have not yet resisted to the point of shedding your blood'
(Hebrews 12:3,4). This struggle also involves a process of disci-
plining by God, who, as our heavenly Father, 'disciplines us for
our good, in order that we may share his holiness' (v.10). For
our part we are expected to invest all our effort and energies
into responding to God's call and discipline: 'Therefore lift your
drooping hands and strengthen your weak knees, and make
straight paths for your feet, so that what is lame may not be put
out of joint, but rather be healed' (vv.12,13). Growth in holiness
is not easy, neither is it automatic or guaranteed. It is clearly a
process that can be shipwrecked, unless we are diligent and
aware of the many ways in which we can stumble: 'See to it
that no one fails to obtain the grace of God; that no root of
bitterness springs up and causes trouble, and through it many
become defiled' (v.15).

So far, most (though not all) evangelicals could have agreed
with this description of struggle; it is when we move into the
area of the inner conflict between the old unredeemed nature
and the new regenerate nature given by God that the cracks –
even chasms – begin to appear. These divisions can be illustrated by the different understandings of Paul's description of
inner conflict in Romans 7:14–25 where he cries out, 'Wretched
man that I am! Who will rescue me from this body of death?'
(v.24). Is he speaking about himself as a mature Christian
believer? 'Yes', answer the Reformers, the Puritans and those

---

[17] ibid., p. 53.

evangelicals who adopt this position (which may be called the 'classic' evangelical view). He is speaking, they claim, of a present inner struggle as he strives for Christian holiness – and it is an intense awareness of conflict which he portrays: 'I do not understand my own actions . . . nothing good dwells within me . . . I can will what is right, but I cannot do it . . . I delight in the law of God in my inmost self, but I see in my members another law at war with the law of my mind, making me captive to the law of sin that dwells in my members.' There is no deliverance or relief from this daily struggle for the Christian – indeed, if a calm seems to have descended, this 'classic' view would ask whether there was any real desire for holiness still present.

J. C. Ryle was clear where he stood about Romans 7 – foursquare with the 'classic' position:

> Paul says nothing in this chapter which does not precisely tally with the recorded experience of the most eminent saints in every age . . . We may take comfort about our souls if we know anything of an inward fight and conflict. It is the invariable companion of genuine Christian holiness . . . May we never forget that without fighting there can be no holiness while we live, and no crown of glory when we die![18]

Perfection this Side of Heaven

But John Wesley had believed differently! He was convinced that the 'wretched man' of Romans 7, who was struggling against sin, was not Paul the Christian, but Paul in his sinful, pre-conversion state. For Wesley, the true goal of religion is holiness, and central to his understanding of the Christian faith was that perfection is attainable in this life – such that the struggle of Romans 7 gives far too pessimistic a view if it is seen as descriptive of the Christian. In particular, he saw sanctification as a second and distinctive work of the Holy Spirit in the individual, akin to the Spirit's work in justification. This work

[18] ibid., pp. xii, 56, 67. For a detailed exposition of the 'classic' interpretation of Romans 7 see J. I. Packer, *Keep in Step with the Spirit* (Leicester, IVP 1984), pp. 263–70.

is received by faith, and is likely to be instantaneous, subsequent to conversion and, hopefully, before death (when it will inevitably happen for all who are born again). Its effect is the eradication of all sinful motivation through the presence of the Spirit, of whose working the individual is consciously aware. He did not teach, contrary to the accusations of many, that such a fully sanctified Christian would never do any wrong after experiencing this work of God's grace.

This teaching was debated frequently within early Methodism, and often misunderstood by both Methodists and others. John Wesley, whose views on the subject fluctuated somewhat over time, summarized his position in his book *A Plain Account of Christian Perfection*, in which he quotes from his teaching over a period of fifty years. The work concludes with the following points, originally written on 27th January 1767:

> Some thoughts occurred to my mind this morning about Christian Perfection, and the nature and time of receiving it, which I believe may be useful to set down.
>
> (1) By perfection I mean the humble, gentle, patient love of God and our neighbour, ruling our minds, words and actions. I do not include an impossibility of falling from it, either in part or in whole. Therefore, I retract several expressions in our hymns, which partly express, partly imply, such an impossibility.
>
> And I do not contend for the term sinless, though I do not object against it.
>
> (2) As to the manner, I believe this perfection is always wrought in the soul by a simple act of faith, consequently, in an instant.
>
> But I believe a gradual work, both preceding and following that instant.
>
> (3) As to the time, I believe this instant is generally the instant of death, the moment before the soul leaves the body.
>
> But I believe it may be ten, twenty or forty years before.
>
> I believe it is usually many years after justification, but that it may be within five years or five months after it. I know no conclusive argument to the contrary.

Many scholars see Wesley's view of perfection as a manifestation of Enlightenment thinking that looks for the attainable goal; it was 'a kind of spiritualized eighteenth-century optimism'.[19] It was a vision of the Christian life which Wesley held from way before his conversion experience, and, as such, it has often been seen as reflecting a more Catholic approach to spirituality than one that is based on a thoroughgoing evangelical theology. He certainly valued the ideas of Catholic as well as Protestant writers, and there is much justification in seeing his approach as a fusing of Protestant ideas of grace with a Catholic vision of holiness. It has also been pointed out that Wesley's view of perfection rested on an incomplete view of sin – it failed to deal with sins of omission.

Given the evident confusion in his own, and his followers', understanding of this teaching, it is not a position that has stood well the test of time. In subsequent Methodism it has been severely modified and, never having taken the field within evangelicalism as a whole, the idea of the eradication of all sinful desire from the heart of the believer while on this earth has very little foothold in any major variety of evangelical spirituality today.[20]

---

[19] Henry D. Rack, *Reasonable Enthusiast*, p. 168.

[20] Henry Rack offers this interesting judgement on Wesley as an evangelical theologian: 'a High Churchman led almost accidentally by his own quest for holiness into leadership of a semi-popular religious movement in areas subject to gradually accelerating social change. Methodist teaching as Wesley visualized it was by no means a conventional form of evangelicalism, because perfection rather than justification became the real centre of his concern. As a device for dealing with the peculiar problems of the kind of people he was ministering to it worked rather well, as an ideal for cheerful ascetics making the world their monastery. But because Wesley failed to capture the Church of England at large and indeed founded a movement which separated from that church, there was never any likelihood that his theology would become significant and central even in England. Intellectually flawed though it may be, it remains of interest as the product of a special set of circumstances in the eighteenth century in a body which managed to avoid a narrow sectarianism, though the perfectionist legacy as such tended to become sectarian in other bodies.' ibid., p. 409.

Rest, not Struggle

If Wesleyan views of holiness failed, in the long run, to dent the 'classic' view of holiness, there arose a nineteenth-century development which has substantially affected views of holiness within evangelicalism right through to the present day.

For the first hundred years, since the beginnings of the eighteenth-century Evangelical Revival, the searching questions about holiness were not resolved. Cannot the God who saved us by grace, with no effort on our part, not do the same for us when it comes to sanctification? Is not any other approach less than consistent – even faithless, in fact? Is not sanctification through faith by grace the only reasonable partner for justification by faith?

In the mid-nineteenth century these unresolved questions were about to receive a fresh answer. Various factors were conspiring to bring this about. At the time the evangelical cause within the Church and the nation was struggling; much of the well-established mid-Victorian ideas of gradual progress and accomplishment were giving way to the newer ideas of Romanticism;[21] and many, especially evangelical clergy within the Church of England, were longing for a deeper experience of the power of God in their lives. There had been an answer developing in America since the 1830s which seemed to offer some very welcome and appropriate answers to these yearnings and uncertainties. After the seeds were sown at several conferences by visiting American speakers, the British 'higher life' movement germinated and began to grow into a very English version of evangelical spirituality.

From the beginning this was identified, in the main, with the Keswick Convention, founded by Canon Harford-Battersby, the vicar of St John's in Keswick, in 1875. Canon Battersby himself had first come into contact with this 'higher-life' or 'deeper-life' teaching at a conference which he attended in Oxford in

---

[21] This was the shift in ways of thinking and perceiving which were greatly influenced by the Romantic poets who were enormously popular in Victorian England – Coleridge, Byron, Scott, Wordsworth. Love of nature, sentimentalism, the longing for the 'ideal', the importance of feeling and intuition, etc., were some of the main ingredients of Romanticism. On the connections between Romanticism and the Holiness Movement see Bebbington, op. cit., pp. 167–9.

1874, the invitation to which had said, 'In every part of the country, the God of all grace has given to many of his children a feeling of deep dissatisfaction with their spiritual state.' Although the main speakers at this conference were American, it was a talk by another Church of England clergyman, Evan Hopkins, that most immediately caught Harford-Battersby's interest. He was speaking about the nobleman who asked Jesus to heal his son. Hopkins taught that 'the nobleman who came to Christ on behalf of his son had real faith. But it was a seeking faith, carrying a burden . . . Seeking faith may be intensely earnest, importunate and persevering, but may exist with great distress, anxiety and worry . . . But the nobleman arrived at a point which may be called a crisis . . . He passed from a *seeking* faith to a *resting* faith. Immediately the step was taken his burden rolled away, his anxiety was gone. Relief came, and a calm peace filled his soul . . . That single step changed the attitude of his faith. It was no longer seeking with a burden. But *resting* without a burden.'

Harford-Battersby was stirred to respond, 'I said to myself, has not my faith been a seeking faith when it ought to have been a resting faith? And if so, why not exchange it for the latter? And I thought of the sufficiency of Jesus and said I *will rest* in him – and I did rest in him.'[22]

Evan Hopkins, like some of the other early Keswick speakers, was not noted for careful and scholarly exposition of the scriptures, as this somewhat fanciful example indicates, but within a decade the movement counted among its leaders Handley Moule, a future Bishop of Durham, who brought much more careful scholarship to its use of the Bible. Like many evangelicals, he had resisted the new teaching at first but, in 1885, while still Principal of Ridley Hall (a newly-formed evangelical theological college in Cambridge), was seeking for a new quality of holiness: 'I had begun to feel, after my years of converted life and ministerial work, guilty of discreditable failures in patience and charity and humbleness. I knew that I was not

[22] J. C. Pollock, *The Keswick Story* (London, Hodder and Stoughton 1964), pp. 26f. Canon Harford-Battersby grew up in Bristol, and by one of the small links that history often makes, he spent most of his childhood in the family home, Stoke House near Clifton. This building is now Trinity Theological College where the present author is Principal.

satisfied and I knew that I ought to find what would satisfy me.'[23] His longing was not for some internal spiritual experience but for new holiness within his life. In September of that year he discovered the answer to his searching within the message of the Keswick movement. Later, after becoming Bishop of Durham, he explained the essentials of Keswick teaching under the heading, 'Holiness by Faith'. He speaks of the difference in a Christian who has discovered the truth of the 'deeper life' in his experience:

> The Christian overcomes the tempter, in the deep secret of the matter, only by calling on him who overcame the tempter for us. The escape from evil, at the centre, in the depth, at the first springs of thought and will, is reached only so . . . Faith welcomes the Lord himself, in an immediate spiritual presence, to reside and, of course, to reign in the heart. And faith commits to that divine resident the management of the troubled inner world.
>
> Thus, looking at the rule and habit of life, this Christian man, not less diligent, humble, watchful, prayerful than before, now, in a way and measure not fully known before, met temptation with the supreme antidote of Christ. His instinct was now, when the evil presented itself, whatever it might be, not so much to struggle with it as to take refuge from it in Christ; not to deal with it by himself, but to give himself over to be managed by his Lord. And great, veritable, blissful, was the difference which came thus to his inner man.[24]

And again, Romans 7 appears on the scene! In 1879 Handley Moule had written a commentary on the Epistle to the Romans in which he had held to the 'classic' position in his understanding of Romans 7:14–25 – namely, that it spoke of the 'one who has so felt the absolute sanctity of God and of his law as to see sin in the *slightest* deviations of will and affection'.[25] He sees it

[23] James Gordon, *Evangelical Spirituality*, p. 206.

[24] Handley Moule and others, *Holiness by Faith: a manual of Keswick Teaching* (London, The Religious Tract Society 1906), pp. 24f.

[25] Handley Moule, *Romans* (Cambridge 1879), p. 131.

as the portrait of a mature Christian who knows the intense daily inner struggle and conflict with his own sinful nature.

In 1894, after his new spiritual awakening, he wrote another commentary on Romans, and now his interpretation expresses the 'Keswick' position. The person described is a Christian who is not living in the power of the Spirit and who consequently must live with the ever-present awareness of failure, defeat, sorrow, frustration and heaviness.[26] He points out the frequent use of 'I' in Romans 7, and the corresponding absence of reference to the Holy Spirit, who becomes the dominant subject in chapter 8 where we read of the freedom of life in the Spirit. Chapter 7, in Moule's latter view, is evidence of the failure that awaits Christians who seek to live in their own strength rather than relying by faith on the victory which the Holy Spirit works in all those who yield to Christ in their pursuit of holiness.

Keswick teaching differed from Wesley's in several specific ways – indeed, the Keswick speakers were very concerned to disassociate themselves from any suggestion of 'Christian perfection'. They did not teach that evil was eradicated from the heart, but that the power of sin has been radically broken – 'never faultless in this world, we may yet be blameless'.[27] Holiness and sanctification are to be focused on 'resting in Christ', not on human effort. A certain quietism was evident: the phrase, 'Let go and let God', become a well-loved catchphrase. Seeking holiness in 'the energy of the flesh' was seen as one of the main mistakes of the Christian. Rather, by faith, one can enter into a conscious awareness of being dead to sin and continually aware of the inner power of the Spirit to transform one's life from a continual falling into sin into a victorious experience of holiness. The dangers of passivity and élitism were not avoided by everyone in the early years – or since.

In the first decade or so of the Convention's life there were two clear issues which differed radically from the 'classic' posi-

---

[26] Handley Moule, *Epistle to the Romans* (London, 1894) p. 195.

[27] F. B. Meyer, the only Baptist minister who became a regular established Keswick speaker in the first quarter-century of the Convention's history, 'Christian Holiness and the conflict with temptation' in *Holiness by Faith*, p. 74. Behind this phrase lies a similar view of sin to the one present in Wesley's teaching – 'Keswick' holiness dealt with conscious sins and not the sinful attitudes and actions of which one was unaware.

tion – holiness comes through rest, not struggle, and usually suddenly rather than gradually:

> In those early years there were many testimonies of a practical deliverance from the power of besetting sin, a constant and lasting blessing found in the keeping power of Christ, which formed so new and blessed an experience, that many spoke of it as a 'second conversion'. Though that phrase was never adopted by the speakers, nor given any official approval, yet it was one quite natural under the circumstances, especially in view of the exactly similar way in which the two blessings came to be received. These Christian people knew quite well, that it was by simple faith in Christ, when their own powers and efforts had proved worthless, that the blessing of pardon and peace had been bestowed upon them; and now it was a real repetition of the same steps that brought them this further blessing . . . No wonder then, that with so much alike in the need, in the Deliverer, and in the condition of faith, they should express the blessing received as a 'second conversion' or more often a 'second blessing'. It was no denial that many more blessings might follow, but only a thankful confession of the very marked and real change effected by this grace of God.[28]

As a result of more eirenic and modified approaches, and particularly the leadership of the Bishop of Durham, 'Keswick' teaching was assimilated into the main stream of evangelical spirituality by the beginning of the present century. In 1892 Bishop Ryle had led in prayer from the convention platform (though this was his one and only attendance, and that on the occasion when Moody was speaking), and by 1900 the Islington Clerical Conference, previously a fierce opponent, now expressed general agreement with the modified 'Keswick' position. To the concern for 'holiness by faith' the convention had added a very strong emphasis on the call to Christian service and to overseas mission in particular. Following these adjust-

---

[28] Hubert Brooke, 'Christian Holiness and Evangelical Work' in *Holiness by Faith*, pp. 136–7.

ments on both sides, the 'Keswick' approach (rather than a specific systematic corpus of teaching) 'shaped the prevailing pattern of evangelical piety for much of the twentieth century'.[29]

The 'classic' position of holiness has remained present within evangelicalism, but not as a controlling theology. Many accept the 'classic' exposition of Romans 7, seeing it as a healthy dose of realism to inject into their conviction that Christ does invite us to discover progressively more of the victory over sin, as we learn to rely more on the indwelling power of the Holy Spirit. In terms of the Movement's motto, many evangelicals would be happy to change, 'Let go and let God' to 'Trust God and get going!'[30] But on the whole, the 'classic' and Puritan coherent theology of holiness sits to one side of mainstream evangelicalism, which has been more eclectic and developmental in its spirituality over the decades.

Some of the differences of approach are, of course, attributable to personality, and the particular life-experiences of an individual – as well as being moulded by the brand of evangelicalism in which one was nurtured. But in essence, the 'classic' view is the theology of a particular period, whereas evangelicalism has developed and been moulded through the different periods of its history. Indeed, many of those who have contended strongly for the 'classic' view on holiness have been of a somewhat culturally conservative bent – this was true of Bishop Ryle, and even more so of Charles Spurgeon. Evangelicalism in its broader scope has seen its spirituality develop both in reaction to, and influenced by, various cultural influences – a process which continues to the present day. Consequently, evangelical theology is a more open-ended system than Puritanism, and has progressively taken on board a wider breadth in spirituality, always conscious that there are clear biblical controlling norms by which to judge any new developments in piety, and that puritanism is one of the clearest and most coherent expressions of a biblical theological system which has more than once acted as a corrective against fanaticism and unrealistic romanticism.

---

[29] Bebbington, *Evangelicalism in Modern Britain*, p. 151.

[30] This substitution is suggested by Jim Packer (*Keep in Step with the Spirit*, p. 157). Packer takes a more exclusive position about the classic view of holiness than I here suggest is common in most evangelicalism.

Is it More Than the 'Language of Zion'?

One of the frustrations that many have found with evangelical spirituality has been what they see as its 'vagueness', its tendency to speak in generalities and high-sounding spiritual phrases that seem to have so little value that they often sound nothing more than 'mere jargon'. The broad 'Keswick' approach illustrates this well. The concern is not so much to spell out the specifics of holiness (indeed, when this has happened a rather taboo-ridden legalism has sometimes crept in), as to deal with the spiritual conditions and attitudes that lie behind all our actions. Change from sinful patterns to a new quality of holiness is what is in view, as is seen in the famous observation of Moody who had previously met a Scottish minister whom he thought, 'the most cantankerous Christian I had ever met'. This was Moody's forthright description of Dr Cumming who, in somewhat surly mood, subsequently attended the Keswick Convention (in 1882) where he discovered God in a fresh way. He said that, almost for the first time, he was aware of the joy of the Lord. Moody met him some years later and was aware of a change. 'Whatever has happened to Cumming?' he asked. 'I have never seen a man so altered, so full of the love of God.' On being told of the transformation which dated from his attendance at the Keswick Convention, Moody, who had not been a Keswick enthusiast, remarked, 'Then I only wish all other Christians would go to Keswick too, and get their hearts filled with the love of God.'

For Cumming, as for countless others, this teaching about holiness led to a transformed life – an observable, and welcome, growth in Christlikeness. Here lies the proof that evangelical holiness is not content to be a matter of pious feelings and devotional experience: it is about lives radically transformed. Yet the fact remains that, sometimes, there seems a lack of 'relatedness' to the practical issues of everyday life – a 'non-relatedness' which, without the necessary personal assimilation and specific response by the individual or community, remains the soothing inoculations of a spiritual gnosticism and the consoling securities of a spiritual sub-culture.

A Fortress Mentality

If the holiness movement infected a certain air of 'non-related-ness' into evangelicalism, another nineteenth-century development was adding a strand of holiness teaching which could be called 'radical avoidance', or, more evocatively, 'a fortress mentality', and yet more damningly, 'a ghetto mentality'.

Sankey's hymn book, *Sacred Songs and Solos*, had as its first hymn what became the signature tune of this mentality – it was enormously popular in late Victorian England:

> Fierce and long the battle rages,
> But our help is near:
> Onward comes our great Commander,
> Cheer, my comrades, cheer!

> 'Hold the Fort, for I am coming!'
> Jesus signals still;
> Wave the answer back to heaven,
> 'By thy grace we will!'[31]

This hymn, written by Philip Bliss, himself a gospel singer, reflects an incident in the American Civil War when the General encouraged his troops to hold the fort. It expressed well the 'radical avoidance' strand in holiness teaching which was greatly encouraged by premillennialist teaching which for a time became a dominant theme in evangelicalism. The world around the Church (the fortress) was so clearly dashing headlong towards evil and destruction that, in order to avoid contamination, one had to raise the drawbridge, defend the barricades – and all too easily, of course, become a ghetto!

The new premillennialism, which emerged from the 1820s onwards, taught (as its own version of an interpretation of Revelation 20 popular with many of the early Fathers of the Church – e.g., Justin, Irenaeus and Tertullian) that Christ would return in person before the millennium in which he would reign with

---

[31] Verse 4 and the chorus. A mark of its popularity can be seen in one of Lord Shaftesbury's remarks at the farewell meeting for Moody and Sankey in 1875: 'If Mr Sankey has done no more than teach the people of England to sing *Hold the Fort*, he has conferred an inestimable blessing on the British Empire.'

his saints for a thousand years before the consummation of all things. They saw the age of the Church as 'the last days' which were degenerating into greater and greater wickedness which would be ended by the sudden, unexpected, visible and physical return of Christ. This view took particularly strong hold in evangelical Anglicanism, and reached its most developed and esoteric form in the teaching of the Plymouth Brethren (a version known as dispensationalism). Its popularity was greatly fostered by being taken up by Moody and Sankey – Moody always gave one address on the premillennial coming of Christ in his crusades. Premillennialism was an innovation of nineteenth-century evangelicalism which held particularly strong sway in the movement for about a hundred years.

As the controlling view of history, it largely replaced the received Protestant orthodoxy of postmillennialism, in which the millennium was seen as a future, glorious age of the Church which would precede the return of Christ and the Last Judgement. This was a great influence alongside the Enlightenment and Victorian views of progress, but as this increasingly became a more secular vision, evangelicals began to abandon it in droves in the latter part of the last century. With it went much of the approach to society which had led people like Wilberforce to adopt a vigorous and progressive social holiness in his campaign for the abolition of slavery. Now the world was seen as a wholly defiling environment out of which individual Christians had to withdraw – 'radical avoidance'. On the other hand, the expectation of the imminent return of the Lord was an urgent motivation to holiness – one needed to be ready at any moment. Similarly it was a spur to lead others to Christ, for tomorrow may be too late, not only through the possibility of early death (a more common feature a century ago than now), but also because world history will soon end. It thus led to a strengthening of the commitment to both evangelism and holiness, but also created a deep distrust of the world, and a holiness which was world-denying and taboo-ridden – taboos which became like identity badges of holiness.

In the second half of the present century the prevalent view has been swinging back, either to a form of postmillennialism, or to a view similar to that held by Augustine and most of the Reformers – amillennialism. This holds that the millennium is not literally a thousand years, but the present age since the time of Christ, in which we look for signs of the present reign of Christ in his Kingdom, which at some future date, which cannot be calculated, will be consummated at the Parousia and the Last Judgement. This view has coincided with a 'letting down of the barricades' and an 'emerging from the ghetto' which has fostered a more socially-orientated vision of the mission of the Church, and a more world-affirming understanding of holiness, in which many of the old taboos, such as drink, dancing, and the theatre, have lost their inevitable power to corrupt.

A Prayer for Holiness

For all the changes and disagreements that have surrounded the evangelical visions of holiness, the desire to become more Christlike has been the prayer at the heart of its spiritual tradition. The exposition of the evangelical view of holiness given earlier in this chapter (in either its nine- or ten-point version) reveals an intensity of commitment to become holy for the sake of Christ. A person must be in earnest about holiness. The spirituality of new beginnings is precisely that – a new life has begun, and every nook and cranny of daily living is subject to the searching work of God's Spirit as he seeks, with our active co-operation, to bring to birth in each of us the characteristics of perfected humanity. From evangelicalism's early years Charles Wesley provides a prayer that expresses this intensity of commitment to the life of holiness:

> I want a principle within
> Of jealous, godly fear,
> A sensibility of sin,
> A pain to feel it near.
>
> I want the first approach to feel
> Of pride or fond desire,
> To catch the wandering of my will,
> And quench the kindling fire.
>
> That I from thee no more may part,
> No more thy goodness grieve,

The filial awe, the fleshly heart,
The tender conscience, give.

Quick as the apple of an eye,
O God, my conscience make;
Awake my soul when sin is nigh,
And keep it still awake.

O may the least omission pain
My well instructed soul,
And drive me to the blood again
Which makes the wounded whole.

6

THE GOD WHO SPEAKS

When we walk with the Lord,
In the light of his Word,
What a glory he sheds on our way.

John Wesley's singleness of purpose expresses well the place of the Bible within evangelical spirituality. 'Let me be *homo unius libri*' (a man of one book).

'Bibliolatry' (the worship of the Bible), is how some critics describe evangelicalism. Though some of its more fundamentalist and unthinking extremes do at times approach perilously near to this position, as a judgement on mainsteam evangelicalism it is as undeserved as it is undiscerning. But the Bible does undoubtedly occupy a place of high honour and esteem. There is a love for the Bible which may at times seem extravagant to some, but it remains love and reverence, not worship. There is that deep affection and excitement for the Word of God that echoes emotions seen long ago in the psalmist. Psalm 119, which is punctuated with expressions of delight and love for God's Word, conveys well the attitude to the Bible that pulsates through the full range of evangelical spirituality:

> I will delight in your statutes; I will not forget your word. (16) ... My soul is consumed with longing for your ordinances at all times. (20) ... Your decrees are my delight, they are my counsellors. (24) ... I find my delight in your commandments, because I love them. (47) ... Oh, how I love your law! It is my meditation all day long. (97) ... How sweet are your words to my taste, sweeter than honey to my mouth! (103) ... Truly I love your commandments more than gold, more than fine gold. (127) ... With open

mouth I pant, because I long for your commandments. (131) ... My lips will pour forth praise, because you teach me your statutes. (171)

Anne Steele (1716–78), one of the earliest of the many evangelical women hymn-writers, extols the scriptures with the same loving enthusiasm that we see in the psalmist.

> Father of mercies, in thy Word
> What endless glory shines!
> For ever be thy Name adored
> For these celestial lines ...
>
> Oh, may these heavenly pages be
> My ever dear delight!
> And still new beauties may I see,
> And still increasing light.

For many evangelicals this love for the Bible is one of the main tests of true discipleship. Although he expresses a degree of exclusiveness about the Bible in determining the state of a person's salvation which many evangelicals today would not want to own, J. C. Ryle insisted that love for the scriptures is at the heart of true Christianity, and in this he was striking, albeit somewhat stridently, a fervent conviction widely held about the supreme value of the Bible for spiritual health and vitality.

> There never was a man or woman truly converted, from one end of the world to the other, who did not love the revealed will of God ... Show me a person who despises Bible reading, or thinks little of Bible preaching, and I hold it to be a certain fact that he is not yet 'born again'. He may be zealous about forms and ceremonies. He may be diligent in attending sacraments and daily services. But if these things are more precious to him than the Bible, I cannot think he is a converted man. Tell me what the Bible is to a man, and I will generally tell you what he is. This is the pulse to try, – this is the barometer to look at, – if we would know the state of the heart. I have no notion of the Spirit dwelling in a man and not giving clear evidence of his presence. And I believe it to be a signal evidence of

the Spirit's presence when the Word is really precious to a man's soul.[1]

In a more reflective mood, we must acknowledge that there are broader indicators of a person's spiritual temperature – in particular, a corresponding love for sharing with God's people in the eucharistic meal. Nevertheless, love of the scriptures will always be a distinctive feature within evangelical spirituality; it is indeed one of the defining marks of the tradition.

A Prominent Place

The Bible's prominence derives from its supreme authority as the wholly trustworthy revelation of God, and the reliable guide to which all other authorities (including tradition, experience and human reason) must submit and against which they will be judged. The ever-present, and ever-open, Bible of evangelicalism derives from the Bible's own teaching of the pivotal importance of the Word of God in the life of faith. A popular expression of this could read as follows:

(1) *The Bible is foundational* as it is the way in which the Spirit brings a person to new birth. 'You have been born anew, not of perishable but of imperishable seed, through the living and enduring word of God' (1 Peter 1:23).

(2) *Faith is first evoked by hearing the Word of God*, which gives us the revelation without which we cannot know him. 'So faith comes from what is heard, and what is heard comes through the word of Christ' (Romans 10:17).

(3) *Without the scriptures we can gain no clear understanding of the nature and purpose of God;* they are the source of spiritual wisdom. 'I have more understanding than all my teachers, for your decrees are my meditation' (Psalm 119:99).

(4) *The Bible is an active and powerful agent for change* within the individual, the community of faith, and society as a whole. The scripture is not merely a library of source documents and information for our own edification;

[1] J. C. Ryle, *Practical Religion*, p. 87.

rather, as God's Word, it is 'living and active, sharper than any two-edged sword' (Hebrews 4:12).

(5) *The Bible is daily sustenance*, vital for spiritual health and well-being: 'One does not live by bread alone, but by every word that comes from the mouth of God' (Matthew 4:4).

(6) *It is the way to formation in holiness.* We cannot rely upon our own ideas of right and wrong; they are a flawed and unreliable guide. 'How can young people keep their way pure? By guarding it according to your word' (Psalm 119:9).

(7) *It is the primary reference point for guidance.* It sets the main parameters for direction in life and discernment of God's will. 'Your word is a lamp to my feet and a light to my path' (Psalm 119:105).

(8) *It is necessary in overcoming temptation* and the attacks of the devil. As Jesus discovered in the wilderness temptation, so his followers need to look to 'the sword of the Spirit which is the Word of God' (Ephesians 6:17).

(9) *It contains the good news to be shared with others.* The gospel is given to us, not invented by us. It has an authority and authenticity in which we can be confident. 'I am not ashamed of the gospel: it is the power of God for salvation to all who believe' (Romans 1:16).

(10) *It is the Word of God which kindles hope throughout the Christian pilgrimage.* It is one of the main means of grace given to us. 'For whatever was written in former days was written for our instruction, so that by steadfastness and the encouragement of the scriptures we might have hope' (Romans 15:4).

A Dominant Place?

On the basis of the Bible's own testimony about itself, and in line with the attitude of Jesus to the scriptures of his day, evangelical spirituality has always given a prominent place to the scriptures and, from the earliest days, there developed a distinctive stance on the Bible. To begin with, however, there were no major formal differences on the question of the Bible's inspiration and authority: it was a difference of emphasis and style that distinguished the evangelicals who stressed, as others generally did not, the Reformation commitment to *sola scriptura* and *sola gratia*. In the prevailing 'reasonable' religion that dominated much of the early eighteenth-century church life, the evangelical approach to scripture had a different feel and emphasis about it rather than a distinctive doctrinal position.

The general latitudinarian temper of the time emphasized the place of reason and reasonableness within religion. There was broad acceptance of a reductionist view that held as important the minimum number of essential doctrines, and many were concerned that Christianity should not be presented as too demanding or burdensome. Morality was the prime concern of religion – it was this that enthused many of the preachers of the Georgian Church. John Wesley did, of course, share many of the prevailing attitudes – he was very concerned with both reason and morality – and most in his day would have been content with his own view of scripture:

> A most solid and precious system of divine truth. Every part thereof is worthy of God; and all together are one entire body, wherein is no defect, no excess. It is the fountain of heavenly wisdom, which they who are able to taste prefer to all writings of men, however wise, or learned, or holy. An exact knowledge of the truth was accompanied in the inspired writers, with an exactly regular series of arguments, precise expression of their meaning, and a genuine vigour of suitable affections.[2]

Though all would have held a similar doctrine of scripture, the evangelicals held to it with passion, conviction and a degree of exclusiveness which was quite alien to the moderate, even temper of many churchmen of the time. It was what Wesley did with the scriptures that made the difference: his enthusiasm, and the earnestness of his advocacy of the power of its central message to change people's lives – this began to forge a new approach to the Bible. In the two centuries after Wesley this difference of approach has divided evangelicals further from other Christian traditions in the Protestant West, until the mass-

[2] John Wesley, *Explanatory Notes upon the New Testament* (1754. This edition, Epworth Press 1976), p. 9.

ive theological and cultural gulf opened up between two radically different views of the Bible. It is only recently that moves on both sides of this divide have begun to make some rapprochement possible across the chasm which, over the years, has become such a complex divergence of approach, ethos, emotion, culture and theology.

In this process the Bible has seemed to some to move from prominence to dominance – to oust the themes of grace, atonement and holiness from their central place until they slink behind the all-dominant Book. Many have seen evangelicalism as 'the spirituality of the Book'. There have been times in the late nineteenth and earlier twentieth century when this may have seemed an accurate description, but that was more an apparent product of the strenuous battles between conservatives and liberals than a principled shift of the centre of evangelical religion. A short sketch of these battles must suffice to illustrate its impact on the spirituality of the movement.[3]

Charles Simeon represents the acceptance of the foundational prominence of the Bible, rather than its all-consuming dominance, in evangelical spirituality, in the period just before the battles began surrounding the questions raised by nineteenth-century biblical criticism. It was as that conflict began that the difference of approach and prominence, which hitherto had marked out the evangelicals from others, became an increasingly polarized theological difference. Simeon exhibited a reasoned approach to the Bible, typical of his own and earlier ages. He held that 'no error in doctrine or other important matter is allowed; yet there are inexactnesses in reference to philosophical and scientific matters, because of its popular style; but the precise force of a common word is not so importantly, so definitely given, as to make it the bulwark of the argument.'[4]

There was an openness in Simeon's approach to the issues of inspiration, authority and accuracy:

Inspiration in my opinion, was of two kinds, according to necessity, yet ever sufficient to preserve truth: – plenary

[3] For a fuller discussion see Bebbington, *Evangelicalism in Modern Britain*, pp. 86–91; 181–191.

[4] Abner Brown, *Recollections of the Conversation Parties of the Revd Charles Simeon* (London, 1863), p. 100.

inspiration, to reveal those things which man could not know, or which the writer did not know: supervisory inspiration, to watch over the things which the writer did know and to prevent him from going wrong. God did not change a writer's character; if of poetic genius, his writing was poetic; if prosaic and plain, such also was his writing. Nay, perhaps some things might be allowed in the writer which are like error: thus, one would give one order of minute events, and another give another, for this is the fact as we see it. But whenever anything depended on chronological arrangement, then there will be found a perfect agreement.[5]

This approach of reasoned submission to the scriptures and relative openness largely disappeared in succeeding generations of evangelicals who found themselves increasingly on the defensive in the face of the rapidly growing ascendancy of biblical criticism. The methods and presuppositions of biblical criticism were seen as causing the demotion of the scriptures which were then made subject to the higher court of human reasoning, scepticism and ingenuity, a process which, more and more, called into question the Bible's inspiration, accuracy, authority – even supernatural religion itself. As a reaction to this, evangelicalism became increasingly distinctive in its definitions about scripture, no longer permitting itself the luxury of the more expansive approach of Simeon's day – gradually doctrines of infallibility and inerrancy were formalized as *the* evangelical position, though it was not until the latter part of the nineteenth century that these positions became widely and formally adopted.[6]

[5] Simeon, in Brown, op. cit., p. 369.
[6] See Bebbington, op. cit., pp. 90–91. 'With the backing of *The Record*, inerrantism made progress among the Anglican clergy. Nevertheless at a representative clerical meeting in 1861 a majority still favoured the traditional view that there might be biblical inaccuracies on non-religious topics. If Fundamentalism as a theological phenomenon is defined as belief in the inerrancy of scripture, Fundamentalism had not prevailed among Evangelicals by this date. The common supposition of historians that Evangelicals of the mid-nineteenth century and before held, as a deduction from the doctrine of inspiration, that the Bible must necessarily contain no error is quite mistaken. This conviction was a novelty, a Romantic innovation. In the middle years of the century there was no more than a rising tide of Fundamentalist opinion.'

The concern to defend the Bible against the different views of inspiration and authority gaining ground in the Church became an all-absorbing occupation for some. Much of evangelicalism was imbued with a biblicism, and sometimes a literalism, which for decades seemed to overshadow the freedom of grace at the heart of evangelical spirituality within a biblical polemicism. Many of the battles were as necessary as they were inevitable, and many evangelicals today, now less defensive, are as a consequence able to engage in open debate with other opinions with a mutuality that yesterday's leaders could not have envisaged. But the intervening defensive engagements sometimes tapped the reserves of vitality, love and holiness within evangelical spirituality: it was a period that threatened to transform a spirituality of the cross into a cult of the book, but, in the long term, that did not happen. In evangelical spirituality the Bible is prominent and foundational; the dominant position belongs to the grace of God and the power of the cross for a sure salvation and a life of holiness.

Listening to Hear God Speak

In this evangelical spirituality of grace and atonement, the initiative is always with God. 'We love because he first loved us' (1 John 4:19). Consequently, prayer is most naturally seen as our response to God, having listened to him through reading and meditation upon the scriptures. It is this hearing of God in the reading of the Bible that stirs the desire to pray and gives direction and content to that prayer. To take one of the countless testimonies to the place of the Bible in spirituality, this one from George Müller illustrates the priority of grace in the operation of Bible-reading.[7] During a two-month retreat and study leave away from his family in 1841 he made what was for him, a very significant discovery:

Before this time my practice had been, at least for ten years

[7] George Müller of Bristol (1805–1898) is remembered as one of the English evangelical heroes of the life of faith. He is one of the clearest examples of those who 'lived by faith' – an expression which refers to the dependence on God for the provision of our needs for a particular calling or ministry rather than relying on appeals or regular income. On this basis he created an extensive work among orphans.

previously, as an habitual thing, to give myself to prayer, after having dressed in the morning. *Now* I saw, that the most important thing I had to do was to give myself to the reading of the Word of God and to meditation on it, that thus my heart might be comforted, encouraged, warned, reproved, instructed; and that thus, whilst meditating, my heart might be brought into an experimental communion with the Lord ... The result I have found to be almost invariably this, that after a very few minutes my soul has been led to confession, or to thanksgiving, or to inter-cession, or supplication; so that though I did not, as it were, give myself to *prayer*, but to *meditation* yet it turned almost immediately more or less into prayer. When thus I have been for a while making confession, or intercession, or supplication, or have given thanks, I go on to the next words or verse, turning all, as I go on, into prayer for myself or others, as the Word may lead to it; but still continually keeping before me, that food for my own soul as the object of my meditation ...

The difference then between my former practice and my present one is this ... I often spent a quarter of an hour, or half an hour, or even an hour on my knees, before being conscious to myself of having derived comfort, encourage-ment, humbling of soul, etc; and often, after having suf-fered much from wandering of mind for the first ten minutes, or a quarter of an hour, or even half an hour, I only then began *really* to *pray*. I scarcely ever suffer now in this way. For my heart being nourished by the truth, being brought into *experimental* fellowship with God, I speak to my Father, and to my Friend (vile though I am, and unworthy of it!) about the things that he has brought before me in his precious Word.[8]

The underlying principle seen here in Müller's experience is that human awareness of God, and human response to God, is dependent on God's prior activity. We can address God because he has addressed us. Consequently, there is a logic to a daily

---

[8] *Autobiography of George Müller*, compiled by G. F. Bergin (second edition, London 1906), pp. 152f.

devotional pattern that reflects the primacy of God's action, and the consequent response awakened in the believer, by putting Bible reading before prayer. In adopting this daily pattern of prayer informed by Bible reading, reflection and meditation, Müller displays the most commonly practised daily discipline found among evangelicals. Its approach explains, in part, why some are suspicious of the teaching of a more contemplative tradition that it is profitable to begin one's time with God by 'centring down', composing oneself in stillness and silence before God, in order to become aware of his presence. A number of factors contribute to evangelical hesitancy on this point (see further in chapter 8); the central theological concern is that if we look inwards we will see, not God, but very unreliable guidance for our prayers because 'the heart is devious above all else; it is perverse – who can understand it?' (Jeremiah 17:9). This caution, valid in its concern, fails to recognize that the whole of the Christian life is lived daily in response to God's initiative. It is the grace of God in which the believer *stands*; it is the rhythm of the life of faith which is not dependent on some regular and sequential devotional pattern. Whatever we do, we can already be aware of God's initiative because his 'love has been poured into our hearts through the Holy Spirit that has been given to us' (Romans 5:5). It would, therefore, be wrong (and un-evangelical!) to deduce a universal daily pattern from this fundamental theological conviction.

A Divine Encounter

Reading the Bible is a divine encounter. The believer is not merely becoming better informed or even simply more encouraged in the Christian life. The Holy Spirit is at work as much in the living contact between the text and the reader as he was in the process of its original writing – thus Charles Wesley encourages us to pray (in the second verse of his hymn, 'Come, Holy Ghost, our hearts inspire'):

> Come, Holy Ghost, for moved by thee
> The prophets wrote and spoke;
> Unlock the truth, thyself the key;
> Unseal the sacred book.

Rarely do evangelicals articulate what they believe to be happening in this encounter, but Jim Packer's threefold definition of the work of the Spirit in this context probably expresses accurately the generally accepted understanding. Just as the Spirit has been at work in the composition and transmission of the scriptures, so 'three processes now go into the effecting of communication through the Bible, namely authentication, illumination, and interpretation.'[9]

By *authentication* is meant that activity of the Spirit within the mind and response of the individual that brings a clear awareness that what one is reading is a word from God himself. The Spirit by his inner working within the believer is authenticating the reading of scripture as a divine communication. The reader is aware that what is being read is no ordinary book. Though the text is written and read by a human being, and though the words themselves are the normal stuff of human communication, God is speaking to the person who reads, in a way similar to partaking in the eucharist where all the participants and the elements involved are human and ordinary, and yet it is, in a very real sense, a participation in Christ.

Illumination is the process whereby the Spirit enables our dull and twisted minds to comprehend clearly the truth of God, recognizing that by our own unaided reason we fail to understand the mind of God, for his way of thinking is different from ours (Isaiah 55:8). The Spirit is at work in believers individually and corporately so that we have the mind of Christ and have a ready understanding of the things of God (1 Corinthians 2:6–16), but as fallible human beings we continue to need this illumination of the Spirit if we are rightly to hear God through the scriptures. Simeon was emphatic on this point:

> It is not the word that does good; but the Holy Ghost by the Word. If the word wrought anything, its operations would be uniform and universal, or, at least, in a much greater degree than it is now, and people would be benefited by it in proportion to the strength and clearness of their intellect . . . it is not the knowledge of the word that benefits, but the knowledge of Christ in the record. We

---

[9] J. I. Packer, *Keep in Step with the Spirit*, p. 239.

might be able to repeat the whole Bible and perish at the last. Christ must be known by us; and that not speculatively but experimentally.[10]

Interpretation 'is the Spirit's activity, effected through our own labour in exegesis, analysis, synthesis, and application, of showing us what the text means for us as God's present word of address to our hearts.'[11] Although the Spirit's activity is so clearly essential, this in no way implies a passivity on the part of the reader. Hard work, study, and the full employment of all a person's mental capacities are required, as God's way is to co-operate fully with the person he has created and redeemed, using all their gifts, insight, abilities and learning.

How to Meet with God in the Scriptures

With such high expectations of meeting with God in the reading of scripture, there have been countless guides as to how to facilitate this encounter. As a typical example we take an early, but representative, attempt to map out the basic approaches – from Henry Venn (1724–1797), who suggested four rules to be followed in order to derive spiritual benefit from the Bible.[12]

(1) 'Whenever we open the sacred book of God, we should lift up our hearts to him, to teach us the true meaning of what we are going to

---

[10] Charles Simeon, *Horae Homileticae* (third edition 1838), vol. 10, pp. 284f.

[11] Packer, *Keeping in Step with the Spirit*, p. 239.

[12] Henry Venn, *The Complete Duty of Man* (third edition London, 1779), pp. 312–317. Henry Venn, a friend of John Wesley, was vicar of Huddersfield from 1759 to 1771 when he moved, because of ill-health, to become vicar of Yelling, a small parish near Cambridge where he became a valued support for Charles Simeon who said of him, 'In this aged minister I found a father, an instructor, and a most bright example.' His book was one of the most popular evangelical works of the eighteenth century. It was intended as an evangelical counterweight to the even more popular *The Whole Duty of Man*, which had been published anonymously in 1657 and which expressed a more 'works-orientated' approach to Christianity. Henry Venn was also the patriarch of a renowned 'evangelical dynasty'. His son, John (1759–1813), became vicar of Clapham where he was part of the Clapham Sect circle which included Wilberforce; his grandson, Henry (1796–1873), became the first Secretary of the Church Missionary Society (1841–1872) and one of the foremost missionary statesmen of the nineteenth century.

read . . . *We must depend on the Spirit for light and instruction when we read God's word.'* There is a reverence for scripture, an awareness of its otherness. This is clearly not the otherness of a sacred object; the book itself is not held to have any numinous quality, as other traditions may attach to a holy relic or an icon. It is sacred because of the inspired text it contains. Its sacredness is both in its Spirit-inspired composition and in its Spirit-inspired reading. It is the totality of this activity that is sacred. It is sacred because it is the written Word of God, bearing witness to Christ, the living Word of God. It is the words – the words as they begin to speak, the words as they are illuminated by the Spirit to the reader – it is these words made alive by the Spirit that make the Bible a sacred book.

(2) 'A second rule, no less worthy of our constant and careful observation, is to read but a small portion at one time.' Although there has often been the concern for extended and consecutive reading of whole sections of the Bible, this second rule of Henry Venn's emphasizes what kind of activity we are undertaking. We are not primarily seeking to become acquainted with the content of the Bible, though that is valid and important, but to be nourished spiritually. As Jesus recalled in the wilderness, 'One does not live by bread alone, but by every word that comes from the mouth of God' (Matthew 4:4). Bible reading is spiritual food, essential daily and regular sustenance for healthy and balanced Christian growth. Mary Lathbury (1841–1913) composed a short hymn on this theme to be used before Bible Study:

> Break thou the Bread of Life,
> Dear Lord, to me,
> As thou didst break the loaves
> Beside the sea;
> Beyond the sacred page
> I seek thee, Lord;
> My spirit pants for thee,
> O Living Word.

The usual eucharistic reference to the feeding of the five thousand, which is the gospel story behind this hymn, reveals again the equivalence between Bible and sacrament, often becoming the primacy of Bible reading over the eucharist. The Bible is food, and often, food enough. At least, *in extremis*, it was so for Bishop Ryle:

> The man who has the Bible, and the Holy Spirit in his heart, has everything which is absolutely needful to make him spiritually wise. He needs no priest to break the bread of life for him. He needs no ancient traditions, no writings of the Fathers, no voice of the church, to guide him into all truth. He has the well of truth open before him, and what can he want more? Yes! though he be shut up alone in a prison, or cast on a desert island – though he never see a church, or minister, or sacrament again – if he has but the Bible, he has got the infallible guide and wants no other. If he has but the will to read that Bible rightly, it will certainly teach him the road that leads to heaven.[13]

Some evangelicals throughout history, and many more nowadays, would want to give a similar place of importance to other means of grace, in particular to the more sacramental and corporate, but most would generally hold to the central conviction – Bible reading provides the main regular sustenance for growth and maturity in Christ.

(3) 'To exact of ourselves correspondent affections; and if we do not experience them, to lament and bewail the poverty and misery of our condition.' Reading the scriptures to become proficient in Bible knowledge, to become a scholar, an expert in the text, though good and worthy in itself, is not the main purpose in daily Bible reading. When pared down to this, Bible reading ceases to be an encounter between God and the whole person. When it is an exercise of the mind only, no real meeting with God is taking place; it has become merely the mind engaging with certain facts and teachings within the text. Hence Henry Venn's insistence that the affections – our conscience, our will and our emotions – must be engaged. Then, and only then, can it be truly said that we have met with God in the reading of his word.

For Henry Venn, the impact which Bible reading has on the affections of the believer is a reliable indicator of spiritual health

---

[13] *Practical Religion*, p. 81.

or sickness. If the scriptures leave one cold, unaffected, unmoved or unchallenged this is evidence that the activity of the Spirit has for too long been resisted. There is no longer anything within the individual that responds to the voice of the Spirit within the reading of scripture. This, for Venn, is a very miserable condition in which to be, for it is evidence of a breakdown in the primary lifeline of the spiritual support system – the communication between the Spirit within the Word and the same Spirit indwelling the believer. While many would hold that this state of affairs is more a cause for serious self-examination than incontrovertible evidence of spiritual decline, the concern would be general throughout the range of evangelical spirituality – a person's response to the scriptures is the acid test of spiritual well-being.

(4) 'Lastly we must read those portions of scripture most frequently which relate to the subjects of greatest moment.' This sounds plain common sense – and so it is, but behind it lie three important principles:

(i) Alongside scripture there is the need for tradition, reason, interpretation and discernment. Through our God-given powers of reasoning we discriminate about what is important and valuable within the scriptures, and what is of more passing, temporary and historical interest only. The Church's tradition contains much of this inherited wisdom which, together with our own discernment and that of our contemporaries, enables us to apply the scriptures in a way that is relevant to our situations – individual and corporate.

(ii) There are certain parts of scripture which are evidently less valuable than others. To hold to this view is not to lessen the Bible's authority, but, by refusing to defend the indefensible (e.g., that parts of Leviticus are as valuable as the Gospel of St Mark), one has a more cogent and convincing doctrine of biblical authority. In the years since Henry Venn, having passed through the battles for the Bible, evangelicalism is ranged between the two polarities of the reasoned discernment represented by Venn and a non-discerning literalistic fundamentalism. It has been the mark of more extreme fundamentalism to ignore the discernment and discrimination that lie behind Venn's fourth instruction. It is when such discernment is absent that evangelicalism more nearly approaches the bibliolatry of which its critics sometimes accuse it.

(iii) Another important principle in the evangelical use of scripture lies behind Venn's phrase about reading those passages of scripture that 'relate to the subjects of greatest moment'. By this he means, not so much those passages that can be found in the Bible that have immediate relevance to some of the great contemporary issues, but rather to the central truths of the Christian faith. In our experience-centred age, and with the dominance of praxis-orientation in much of our theology, there is a tendency to look in the scriptures for those passages which speak relevantly (however obliquely and loosely) to our situation. This was not the approach which Venn was recommending, nor one that has generally been central in evangelical spirituality. Venn would be concerned that we read and meditate on the great story of our redemption, that we feed on the central truths of the faith. In so doing the truth of scripture, the very mind of God, becomes part of our way of thinking. Over the years of disciplined Bible reading our thought processes are being progressively redeemed and sanctified so that, hopefully, we have an increasing ability to think biblically, theologically and Christianly about life and all the specific contemporary issues that surround us. This difference of approach to the Bible and contemporary issues is one of the main distinctives of the use of the Bible within evangelicalism.

The Individual Quiet Time

The daily time of Bible reading and free prayer, usually called the 'Quiet Time' is, more than any other exercise – individual or corporate – the heart of evangelical spirituality. It usually replaces what others receive through the Daily Office, the daily Eucharist, the hour of silent contemplation, or the more common practice within the Eastern Church of prayer and meditation with an icon. It is a means of grace in which the individual meets with God and is resourced afresh.

It is, in essence, an individualistic exercise – and this has more often been seen as a strength rather than a weakness. We, in the West, live at a time when we are regaining an understanding of the corporate, having passed through several centuries in

which both society and the Church have been glorying in the
benefits of individualism. In the process of this rediscovery, it
would be short-sighted to forget the enormous benefits that
have resulted from this individualism – as we now become aware
of some of its deficiencies. We have enjoyed the advantages of
the freedom and ability of individuals to read, think, discern,
and make their own judgements, rather than believe only what
they are told both to think and to do by some authority in
Church or state. This is one of the long-term fruits of the
Reformation and the Enlightenment; it is certainly one which
has bolstered the evangelical Quiet Time and made it so central
to the daily diet of evangelical spirituality. Every Christian is
encouraged to come to their own understanding, guided by the
scriptures and illuminated by the Spirit. The mind, renewed by
the Spirit, is a precious gift of God for each individual. It
occupies a central place within the evangelical understanding of
the individual before God, and nowhere more than in the use
of the Bible do we see the importance given to the place of the
mind in the life of faith.

In the days when popular books on practical Christianity were
more sparingly published, and consequently lasted for much
longer, R. A. Torrey's[14] manual on Christian living, *How to
Succeed in the Christian Life*, was one that had a wide readership
among evangelical Christians in the early decades of this
century. He spoke of what he saw as the vital benefits of the
healthy individualism of personal Bible reading:

> We live in a day in which false doctrine abounds on every
> hand and the only Christian who is safe from being led
> into error is the one who studies his Bible for himself
> daily. The Apostle Paul warned the elders of the church in
> Ephesus that the time was soon coming when grievous
> wolves should enter in among them not sparing the
> flock . . . He said, 'I commend you to God and to the Word

[14] R. A. Torrey (1856–1928) was one of the American revivalists in the
tradition of Charles Finney and Moody and Sankey who have had a marked
influence on the British evangelical scene. Torrey, with his singer-associate,
C. M. Alexander, led a series of campaigns in the United Kingdom during
1903–1905 similar to those of Moody and Sankey a quarter of a century
earlier.

of his grace, which is able to build you up and to give you an inheritance among them which are sanctified.' Through meditation on the Word of God's grace they would be safe even in the midst of abounding error ... Our spiritual health, our growth, our strength, our victory over sin, our soundness in doctrine, our joy and peace in Christ, our cleansing from inward and outward sin, our fitness for service, all depend upon the study of the Word of God. The one who neglects his Bible is bound to make a failure of the Christian life.[15]

The confident individualism is marked, the Reformation and Enlightenment emphasis being strengthened by the American confidence that nerved evangelicalism in the United Kingdom at a time of low fortunes and which has remained part of evangelicalism's distinctive features to the present day. In Torrey's estimation, the individual and the guidance of the Spirit is a better recipe for orthodoxy in doctrine and soundness of spiritual health than the general diet they are likely to get at the hands of the theological operators of the day. He is happy to commend them to God's grace in their private Bible study: it is a confluence of a very high view of the authority of scripture and the fundamental reliability of an individual indwelt by the Spirit that lies at the heart of evangelical spirituality, and has often annoyed theologians when their learning and scholarship is treated with caution, not to say, contempt; not infrequently, the same powerful combination has led to somewhat fantastic and extravagant theological positions and idiosyncratic, even quixotic, schemes and policies. Its strength is in the dignity it reserves for the individual before God.

This strength of individualism within evangelical spirituality contributes to the iconoclasm and lack of respect for church order and authority figures (like bishops) which is often noted. It may well be that this trait has so been strengthened by the American influences within British evangelicalism, that it contributes to the slightly 'non-British' feel about some features within evangelicalism, which has often been part of the sub-text

[15] R. A. Torrey, *How to Succeed in the Christian Life* (London, James Nisbet and Co. 1906), pp. 46–8.

in some of the criticisms of evangelicalism, at least in England. It would be wrong, however, to over-emphasize the American influence at this point: Charles Simeon was equally clear that the individual Christian reading the scriptures under the guidance of the Spirit 'needs no casuist but an upright heart; no director but a mind bent on doing the will of God'.[16] Returning to Torrey, the self-regulating approach to the spiritual life is so crucial in his judgement, that he declares, with less caution than many (having seen some of its dangers) would advocate today: 'Any day that is allowed to pass without faithful Bible study is a day thrown open to the advent into our hearts and lives of error or of sin.'[17]

He proceeds to outline three possible methods that one could adopt for daily Bible reading. In brief, his second is this:

(1) Read the passage five times, once aloud. Each new reading will bring out some fresh point.

(2) Divide the passage into its natural divisions, giving each its own heading.

(3) Note the important differences between various versions of the Bible (in his day this was just the Authorized and the Revised Versions).

(4) Write out the leading facts of the passage.

(5) Make a note of any persons mentioned and any light thrown on their character.

(6) Note down and classify the principal lessons learnt from the passage.

(7) Find the central truth of the passage.

(8) Find the key verse, if there is one.

(9) Mark and memorize the best verse in the passage.

(10) Write down what new truth you have learned from the passage.

(11) Write down what truth already known has come to you with new power.

(12) What definite thing have you resolved to do as a result of studying this chapter?

---

[16] Charles Simeon, *Horae Homileticae* (21 vols., 1832–3, reprinted Grand Rapids 1988), vol. 15, p. 53.

[17] R. A. Torrey, op. cit., p. 48.

This reveals the seriousness and application expected in the daily Quiet Time, involving as it does many elements of a daily diary or spiritual journal, as well as a personal Bible commentary. And it must be remembered that Torrey was propounding what he expected to be the common discipline of ordinary men and women of all social classes and educational backgrounds. It was the dignity that this individualism gave to each believer, as much as anything else, that has enabled the practice of the Quiet Time to survive even in cultures not known for their reading strengths – it has given control of their spiritual lives into people's own hands, often when other authorities lorded it over them in other spheres of life. For many, however, over the decades since, the individualism, the emphasis on literacy, the discipline, and the time needed, have meant that questions have increasingly been asked about the practice:

– What of the less literate?

– What of those who need a more communal approach to their spirituality?

– Are many not secretly failing in this discipline and living with unnecessary guilt?

– Is it not in danger of being a legalism contrary to the evangelical doctrines of grace and freedom?

These thoughts are now more and more reflected in the popular guides to Bible reading produced in our generation. John Stott writes,

> If there is no single secret, there are no hard and fast rules either. For example, the practices of the daily 'Quiet Time' of Bible reading and prayer, preferably first thing in the morning and last thing at night, is not an inviolable tradition. It has certainly stood the test of time and brought untold profit to many generations of Christians. I myself am old-fashioned enough to retain confidence in it as an extremely valuable discipline. But it is still only a tradition; it has not been laid down in Scripture. So we have no liberty to add it to the decalogue as a kind of eleventh commandment. Nor was such a practice possible before the invention of printing and the availability of cheap Bibles for all. To insist on it as indispensable to Christian living

would be to disqualify the millions of Christians who lived in the first fifteen centuries.[18]

Guidance and the Bible

The dangers of an excessive individualism are most clearly seen in the way some evangelicals have used the Bible in their attempts to discover the specific guidance of God. Torrey clearly felt it necessary to issue a caution:

> Do not make a book of magic out of the Bible. Do not ask God to show you his will and then open your Bible at random and put your finger on some text and take it out of its connection without any relation to its real meaning and decide the will of God in that way. This is an irreverent and improper use of scripture. You may open your Bible at just the right place to find right guidance, but if you do, it will not be by some fanciful interpretation of the passage you find. It will be by taking the passage in its context and interpreting it to mean just what it says as seen in its context. All sorts of mischief has arisen from using the Bible in this perverse way.[19]

In spite of this warning, and many others like it, individuals have continued to make use of the Bible to obtain guidance in exactly the way most leaders caution against. It is an example of the relative importance which individuals ascribe to authority figures in such a 'people's spirituality'.

But then, all leaders have not been so cautious in their own personal search for guidance. This point is well illustrated by the approach to guidance of one of the much-loved evangelical figures in the early part of this century. Bishop Taylor Smith (1860–1938),[20] as he was later to become, was offered two different places for his first curacy – one in Leeds, the other in Upper Norwood in South London:

[18] J. R. W. Stott, *Understanding the Bible* (London, Scripture Union 1972), p. 244.
[19] R. A. Torrey, op. cit., pp. 118f.
[20] Bishop of Sierra Leone (1897–1901), and afterwards Chaplain General to the Forces (1901–1925).

I spent much time in prayer, and again the Lord gave me an answer. I was staying at a friend's house, and coming down in the morning after a sleepless night, seeking for guidance, I took up a small book of texts lying on the table and read thus, 'Give me a blessing, for thou hast given me a south land, give me also springs of water. And he gave me the upper springs and the nether springs.' I wrote immediately to Mr Graham, and accepted his offer, and God gave me a blessing both in the upper springs (Upper Norwood) and nether springs (Lower Norwood). Some may say this was a fanciful interpretation, and so it might have been, but God's blessing was on it, and his Spirit spoke through those words to my soul, and I simply obeyed.[21]

Such approaches were not easily discarded. On being invited to go out to Sierra Leone, for the first stay, as Diocesan Missioner, he continues to exhibit a similar approach to God's guidance:

I lifted my heart in prayer thus – 'Lord, if it be not tempting thee, give me a sign before the day is over. Let me not choose myself, but do thou choose for me.' When I reached home a letter awaited me. Someone who knew not the slightest of the workings of my heart had been prompted to send me the text, 'All things work together for good to them that love God,' and on looking over some papers to find a map of Sydenham, where I was going that evening to take a Scripture Union Meeting, a card dropped out on the carpet, with the words, 'Thus saith the Lord thy Redeemer, the Holy One of Israel; I am the Lord thy God which teacheth thee to profit, which leadeth thee the way thou shouldest go' (Isaiah 48:17).

I was continually wakened in the night by such words coming to my mind as, 'Go forth in this thy might,' and, 'Ye have been my witness in Judea and in Samaria, and now ye shall go to the uttermost part of the earth.' I have

[21] E. L. Langston, *Bishop Taylor Smith* (London, Marshall, Morgan and Scott n.d.), p. 38.

somewhat altered the last, but it is the way it came to my heart. I might take my home in Westmoreland to be Judea. When I came to Norwood, it might truly be deemed Samaria, and now God had said, 'Go to the uttermost parts of the earth.' If further proof were wanted to decide me, it came from the Scripture Union portion, 'Behold, I send an angel before thee to keep thee . . . the place that I have prepared' (Exodus 23:20). I hesitated no longer, but wrote my acceptance at once. I cannot tell you the indescribable peace that took possession of my soul.[22]

Torrey had warned against it, yet countless thousands (including a few more bishops who could be mentioned!) have found that such approaches to guidance have 'worked'. There are a number of reasons that can be adduced to discourage such practices, like the importance of using the God-given gift of reason, and the need to interpret the scriptures contextually, but what can never be commended as a good principle, has not seemed to prevent God, in his providence, from accommodating himself to human simplicity and over-zealousness. Preachers, parents, teachers, authors and spiritual directors always find it incumbent upon them to point out the danger of such ways, and the safety and propriety of sound spiritual judgement. But any spiritual tradition, whichever one it happens to be, would be hiding from reality if it failed to acknowledge those occasions when God seems not to obey the very rules of safety which we impose upon ourselves and others in order to protect his honour!

Group Bible Study

There are two specific elements within the evangelical tradition which act as a framework for its Spirit-inspired individualism; they supplement the lone individual with an open Bible, thus giving a broader and more adequate theology for understanding and discerning the Word of God. They are corporate Bible study and preaching, though they have not both held an equal prominence throughout the history of evangelicalism.

Of the two, corporate Bible study has occupied a much smal-

[22] ibid., p. 53.

ler place within the tradition. The picture of a congregation meeting in small groups, week by week, to study a portion of the scriptures together may seem to many an accurate portrayal of corporate evangelical spirituality – in fact it is a relatively recent development on any scale, and even then, it has always been far from universal. Nevertheless, behind the practice of group Bible study lies a thoroughly evangelical principle – it is through corporate enquiry, in openness to the Spirit, that the people of God are able to understand, discern and apply the word of God.

In general terms, as a common practice, it owes much to two factors – modern developments in education with the emphasis on learning within groups, and the strength of evangelicalism within colleges and universities where, during the last fifty years, group Bible study has usually been the most obvious focus of corporate spiritual life within a peer group of Christian students. This activity has earned for itself an honoured place in the life of many local churches, (especially among young people), often by transference from student models. It has largely replaced the weekly Bible exposition given by the pastor which was a regular feature of many churches before the advent of group learning methods.

Even here, the emphasis within Bible study groups has been changing under the influence of two more recent factors. Newer educational and psychological understandings of group discovery and the impact of charismatic renewal have led to a greater emphasis on personal sharing, mutual prayer support and encouragement – much more reflecting the broader purpose and agenda of the early Wesleyan class meetings.

The rise to prominence of Bible study groups, and the more broadly based fellowship groups, has occurred at a time when the group experience which was formerly prominent in evangelical spirituality has almost totally disappeared – family prayers. While this did not normally take the form of a Bible study as such, it did give a small group context for the hearing of God's word within the family circle (which would have included the household servants in Edwardian, and earlier days!). Usually the father would have given a short devotional comment after reading a passage from scripture which, over the years, would have provided a received biblical framework in the light of which the household was to operate. In its own age, it was a vehicle for the corporate application of the scriptures, though of a somewhat paternalistic kind.

The Place of the Word Preached

Alongside private and corporate Bible study, evangelical spirituality has traditionally placed considerable emphasis on the Word of God, preached and expounded by those whom God has called to this office and ministry. Brownlow North (1810–1875) was a leading figure in the spiritual awakening of 1859 in Scotland – a description of his preaching illustrates the formative role of the sermon in evangelical spirituality.

> So far was there from ever being a lightness in his handling of the scripture, that many times in every service the sense that he was reading and preaching the living word of the living God seemed to be almost overpowering. No high priest in the Holy Place could have handled the Urim and Thummim with greater awe and reverence than this preacher treated the divine oracles. He believed that the word of God was the sword of the Spirit; and the very remarkable effects upon the consciences, understandings, and lives of men, wrought through him by this instrument, fully bore out his belief.[23]

The preaching office is seen as one of the vehicles of the communication of God's word, a means of grace, ordained by God for salvation and edification. Simeon saw preaching as the main means, chosen by God, to ensure a faithful understanding of the scriptures:

> He chiefly uses the ministry of his servants whom he has sent as ambassadors to a guilty world . . . When the centurion also had sought with much diligence and prayer to know the way of salvation, God did not instruct him by his Word or Spirit, but informed him where to send for instruction, and by a vision removed the scruples of Peter

---

[23] K. Moody-Stuart, *Brownlow North* (London, Banner of Truth, reprinted from the 1878 original in 1961), pp. 126f.

about going to him. This was done that the established ministry might be honoured, and the church might look to their authorized instructors as the instruments whom God would make use of for their edification and salvation. Thus it is at this time. God is not confined to means, but he condescends to employ the stated ministry of his Word for the diffusion of divine knowledge.[24]

For evangelicals, it is clearly not sufficient to view the sermon as an interesting, and hopefully stimulating, few minutes in the course of Sunday worship – it is a vital ingredient in the individual's spiritual diet, and evangelical hopes are thus disappointed in worship if the sermon does not provide 'food for hungry souls'. The sermon is part of the essential diet for the nourishment of both corporate and individual spirituality. Its aim, according to Simeon, is 'to humble the sinner, to exalt the Saviour, and to promote holiness',[25] and although this is now often accomplished within the compass of a twenty-minute sermon, for most of evangelicalism's history (and still today in certain traditions) a period of forty-five minutes or more would be seen as more realistic.

As a means of grace, preaching stands alongside the eucharist, for some in prominence before it. It has a sacramental status which the renowned twentieth-century Methodist preacher, W. E. Sangster, explains by making a clear distinction between a sermon and an address. He defines the sermon as 'a sacramental act . . . an address is a man talking to me: a sermon is a man speaking *from God*. The difference between an address and a sermon is deep, basic, and elemental. Any preacher who knows his business knows the difference *in himself*.'[26]

With such a high and sacramental view of the office of preaching, with the presence of God brought to the congregation in such immediacy, the sermon has an assured place within the scheme of evangelical spirituality. It 'is a deed, not of man merely or chiefly, but of God . . . [Preaching] was, is, and ever

[24] Charles Simeon, from a sermon entitled, 'Christ Crucified or Evangelical Religion Described', printed in *Let Wisdom Judge*, p. 103.

[25] Charles Simeon, Preface to *Horae Homileticae*, p. xxi.

[26] W. E. Sangster, *The Craft of the Sermon* (London, Epworth Press 1954), pp. 3f.

will be, God's chief way of announcing his will to the world . . .
Preaching is a constant agent of the divine power by which the
greatest miracle God ever works is wrought and wrought again.
God uses it to change lives.'[27]

Many evangelical approaches to ministry and ordination, understandably, hold preaching to be the central and high point of the
minister's calling – this is especially so in the Reformed tradition, represented here by Robert Murray McCheyne: 'The grand
work of the minister, in which he is to lay out his strength of body
and mind, is preaching. Weak and foolish as it may appear, this
is the grand instrument which God has put into our hands, by
which sinners are to be saved, and saints fitted for glory.'[28]

Given such a calling, a great responsibility rests upon the
shoulders of the preacher. The preacher 'has been sent, he is
a commissioned person, and he is standing there as the mouth-
piece of God and of Christ to address these people.'[29] A
preacher 'mounts his pulpit steps on Sunday knowing he has a
message from the Lord.'[30] With such thoughts in mind, Spurgeon had no hesitation in giving this advice to preachers in
training: 'Get your message fresh from God. Even manna stinks
if you keep it beyond its time; therefore get it fresh from heaven,
and then it will have a celestial relish.'[31] The effectiveness
of preaching, so understood, depends much on the personal
spirituality of the preacher. To be a vehicle of the living word
of God, a preacher must first and foremost be a person who
has heard, and been vitally transformed by, the message before
it is preached to the people. Preaching is 'logic on fire! Eloquent
reason! . . . It is theology on fire . . . Preaching is theology
coming through a man who is on fire . . . I say again that a man
who can speak about these things dispassionately has no right
whatsoever to be in a pulpit; and should never be allowed to
enter one.'[32]

[27] W. E. Sangster, ibid., pp. 4, 11, 16.
[28] Andrew Bonar, *Memoirs and Remains of Robert Murray McCheyne*, pp. 400f.
[29] Martyn Lloyd-Jones, *Preaching and Preachers* (London, Hodder and
Stoughton 1971), p. 53.
[30] W. E. Sangster, op. cit., p. 11.
[31] Charles Spurgeon, *An All-round Ministry* (1900, reprinted, Banner of
Truth Trust 1960), p. 336.
[32] Martyn Lloyd-Jones, op. cit., p. 97.

Charismatic renewal has re-emphasized an important ingredient in the ministry of the sermon, namely the discernment of what God is wanting to say, by the Spirit, through the exposition of the scriptures, to the particular situation of the people present today. There is an essential listening task laid upon the preacher in order to know how to expound God's word in the context of what he is doing among his people and within the world today. David Watson expressed the need for such 'listening preachers':

> We need increasingly today a prophetic note in our preaching ... What is the Spirit saying to the churches? What emphases should we concentrate on? What is the word of the Lord now? There should be an arresting (and no doubt often a disturbing) relevance about the preached word of God.[33]

Though the congregation will do much of this interpretive, prophetic work in their own listening to the sermon, the preacher has the responsibility to lay the foundations for the hearing of God's word with all its contemporary relevance in his or her own preparation.

As with the individual's own times of Bible reading, the sermon is not 'for information only'. It is to bring about a change, a growth in holiness, a furtherance of the work of the Spirit in the individual listener and within the congregation as a whole. It is a creative act. 'Preaching should make such a difference to a man that he is never the same again. Preaching, in other words, is a transaction between the preacher and the listener. It does something for the soul of man, for the whole of the person, the entire man; it deals with him in a vital and radical manner.'[34]

Inevitably, the preacher's high calling and the congregation's high expectations, dependent as they are on the spirituality, gifts and application of individual preachers, produce inconsistent results. Furthermore, it is commonplace to see the present age as a low-point for the sermon within evangelicalism.[35] But

---

[33] David Watson, *I Believe in the Church* (London, Hodder and Stoughton 1978), p. 209.

[34] Martyn Lloyd-Jones, op. cit., p. 53.

[35] For example see John Stott, *I Believe in Preaching* (London, Hodder and Stoughton 1982), pp. 50–89; and Martyn Lloyd-Jones, op. cit., pp. 9–25.

however disappointed people may be by the performance of a particular preacher, it remains part of the lifeblood of evangelical spirituality to be looking to hear God speak – and speak power-fully, and life-transformingly – through the Sunday sermon.

The danger for some congregations is that they exhibit a submissive acceptance of all that is said. Though the more sectarian and super-spiritual groupings seem particularly prone to this, the temper of much modern evangelicalism would take as axiomatic John Stott's reminder to his fellow preachers:

> We claim no infallibility for our interpretations of Scrip-ture. We should urge our hearers to 'test' and 'evaluate' our teaching. We should welcome questions, not resent them. We should not want people to be moonstruck by our preaching, to hang spellbound on our words, and to soak them up like sponges.[36]

For all its importance, preaching remains a vehicle – a means of making the Bible more accessible, a way of opening up the scriptures so that they can perform their vital and foundational role among God's people.

Thus there exists a threefold chord within evangelical spirituality that provides the necessary strength for understanding and obey-ing the Word of God:
– the individual reading his or her Bible under the tutelage of the Holy Spirit;
– the discovery of the truths of the scriptures within the fellowship of believers;
– and the faithful exposition of the scriptures in preaching.

[36] John Stott, ibid., p. 177.

7

THE GOD WHO ACTS

What he says we will do,
Where he sends we will go,
Never fear, only trust and obey.

The seventeenth-century Deists, while small in numbers, had an influence that was still apparent at the time of the eighteenth-century Evangelical Revival. Their view of God has been described as that of 'a constitutional monarch who had signed a constitutional compact and retired from the active government of affairs.'[1]

The evangelical understanding of God could hardly be more different. He is the God who is thoroughly involved in the ongoing life of the world. He is actively concerned in the outworking of peace, righteousness and judgement; he is committed to applying the work of salvation in individuals' lives, and lovingly concerned with the personal needs and aspirations of each believer and the community of faith. This is no more than the classic theistic position, but God's activity and involvement are so strongly part of the daily expectation of evangelical spirituality that immanence, involvement and action are more prominent in evangelical apprehensions of God than transcendence, mystery and inscrutability. This is not to deny the presence of these latter qualities within evangelical experience – God would not be God if glimpses of his essential reality were not apprehended by everyone, whatever their main conscious expectations of God – but those aspects which speak most of God's separateness

---

[1] Leslie Stephen, *History of English Thought*, vol. 2, p. 338, quoted in H. D. McDonald, *Ideas of Revelation* (London, Macmillan 1959), p. 263.

from his creation are less formative in the general thrust of evangelical spirituality.

There are three factors inherent in this view of God which have a major impact on the ethos of evangelical spirituality. A life focused on the God who acts, inevitably becomes itself action-based, with a spirituality that is energetic (as we noted when looking at the effect of assurance in chapter 3), and ever seeking ways of imitating and serving the God of action, wherever his choice may lead. Secondly, this spirituality is one in which intercession dominates the practice of prayer; it is that part of prayer which pleads for change and seeks to co-operate with God as he moves into action. Thirdly, this activity-directed spirituality is deeply conscious of the need to be resourced, strengthened, and empowered for the demanding life of action and service.

Active Service

If God is committed to action, the person who wishes to remain close to him will do so by being involved with him in that activity. Though rarely expressed in this way, this concept is one of the main strands in the evangelical understanding of imitation and identification. God is not simply to be imitated in his holiness, but in his activity.[2] To take one example from many that could be chosen, R. A. Torrey taught that

> One of the important conditions of growth and strength in the Christian life is work. No man can keep up his physical strength without exercise and no man can keep up his spiritual strength without spiritual exercises, i.e., without working for his Master. The working Christian is the happy Christian. The working Christian is the strong Christian. Some Christians never backslide because they are too busy about their Master's business to backslide. Many professed

[2] For examples of how this activism became apparent from the very beginning of the Evangelical Revival and, in particular, how it changed the approach to local church life and ordained ministry see David Bebbington, *Evangelicalism in Modern Britain*, pp. 10–12, 41–2.

Christians do backslide because they are too idle to do anything but backslide.[3]

Spurgeon, in speaking to ministers (with customary hyperbole) passed on the advice, 'Kill yourselves with work, and then pray yourselves alive again.'[4] So much did he long for energetic action in the service of God that he indulges in a revealing wistfulness: 'For my part, I would have remained a young man if I could, for I fear I am by no means improved by keeping. Oh, that I could again possess the elasticity of spirit, the dash, the courage, the hopefulness of days gone by! My days of flying are changed to those of running, and my running is toning down to a yet steadier pace.'[5] Spurgeon, who was often more relaxed than his severe reputation suggests, uses the ironic humour of the preacher to underline the belief that there is no calling more worthy than expending oneself in wholehearted service of Christ. 'To spend and be spent' has been the motto of many. R. W. Dale, a moderate-evangelical contemporary of Spurgeon, expressed, with approval, his more detached observation that, among evangelicals,

> the obligation to 'work is universally recognized . . . public Christian opinion condemns the man or woman who is doing nothing . . . The evangelical saint of today is not a man who spends his nights and days in fasting and prayer, but a man who is a zealous Sunday-school teacher, holds mission services among the poor, and attends innumerable committee meetings.[6]

This commitment to God-imitating activity has two main expressions, usually inseparably intertwined – concern for the socially deprived, and the need for evangelism. The campaigns of Wilberforce, and his evangelical friends, for the abolition of slavery, and Lord Shaftesbury's for the amelioration of the appalling conditions of the young and the poor in work and in housing, are the flagships of evangelical social concern through-

---

[3] R. A. Torrey, *How to Succeed in the Christian Life*, p. 82.

[4] C. H. Spurgeon, *An All-round Ministry*, p. 272.

[5] ibid., pp. 131f.

[6] R. W. Dale, *The Evangelical Revival* (London, Hodder and Stoughton 1880), pp. 35f.

out the eighteenth and nineteenth centuries. This twin concern was evidenced in many of the movements and societies founded in this period, for example, the YMCA and the YWCA founded in 1844 and 1877 respectively. In these, and many other examples, there was a clear commitment to activity, doing God's work, in the interdependent spheres of social concern and evangelism. This dual, but united, commitment to action is reflected in an entry in William Wilberforce's diary in 1787: 'God Almighty has set before me two great objects, the suppression of the slave trade and the reformation of manners.'

When the Church began to see this dual calling as divisible into the two separate concerns of social action and evangelism, evangelicalism (for about half a century or more) showed a distinct, and at times theologically defended, preference for evangelism over social action – except in the overseas mission field where the two remained largely united. In the latter part of the twentieth century, when much of evangelicalism emerged from the entrenched positions which led to this particular division between 'liberal' and 'conservative' Christians, the more unitive and traditional evangelical view of Christian action once more began to remodel basic attitudes and spirituality.

Throughout this whole period, however, the distinctive form of evangelical activism that has remained constant has been the call to 'win others for Christ'. There is no obligation to action more solemnly required of each believer than this. There are no indicators of effective Christian living as clear as proven ability in personal evangelism. This is not an activity that can be left to the professionals alone, for every Christian is called to be a witness and to be ready to give a reason for the hope which is within. Being a 'soul-winner' (a somewhat antiquated but important phrase within the tradition) received particular prominence following the revivalism of the late nineteenth century. 'Personal work', as it is often called, is expected of all believers:

> How can a young Christian bear fruit? The answer is very simple and very easy to follow. You can bear fruit for your Master by going to others and telling them what your Saviour has done for you, and by urging them to accept this same Saviour and showing them how to do it. There

is no other work in the world that is so easy to do, so joyous, and so abundant in its fruitfulness . . . The youngest Christian can do personal work . . . When we were in Sheffield, a young man working in a warehouse accepted Christ. Before the month's mission in Sheffield was over he had led thirty others to Christ, many of them in the warehouse where he himself worked . . . Make up your mind that you will speak about accepting Christ to at least one person every day.[7]

They are words that were, for most, an enormous challenge – maybe so enormous that they produced inaction by their seeming insurmountability. But in our age, the call is still substantially the same. David Watson, the most sensitive of evangelists, sets the vision within a description of the early church:

When we look at the early church, frail with its human fears and failings but alive in the Spirit, we see everyone gossiping the gospel . . . It was the 'little people', the nameless laity – the *idiotes*, as they were later called – who went everywhere preaching Christ. No opposition could stop them. It was the whole church, active in witness and bold in evangelism, that dramatically changed the world of their day.[8]

So often it has been the 'up-front evangelists' who have emphasized this central call to activity for God – often there has not been the rightful distinction made between those who are especially gifted as evangelists and the majority who are not, but who are still called to witness to their faith in word as well as in deed and in lifestyle (David Watson is careful to make this distinction). This has often led to guilt and paralysis in action, at the very point where the individual Christian has longed to be most effective for God; to be one with Christ in his passion to bring others to eternal life. It has become, for some, one of the most enduring disappointments in the whole of their Christian experience. Nowadays, most would feel able to disagree with Torrey's assertion, quoted above, that there is no easier thing

[7] R. A. Torrey, op. cit., pp. 83ff.
[8] David Watson. *Discipleship*, p. 188.

in the world to do than to lead another person to Christ! The difficulties are acknowledged, but the call is still given as a central duty in the spiritual life. David Watson posed the questions:

> How can we overcome the natural reticence, partly cultural, that makes most western Christians like the great Canadian rivers in winter, frozen at the mouth? How can we release our congregations from the natural fear of men and reticence to change? How can evangelism spontaneously flow from our church services and fellowships out into the streets, homes and places of work – where people are?[9]

Much of the approach to training, education, nurture and spiritual growth in evangelical churches is designed to answer these problems. But however sensitive, realistic and discerning may be the approach, it remains one of the inescapable facts about evangelical spirituality that, at the top of its activistic agenda, there lies a commitment to achieve a goal which only some (perhaps not the majority) fulfil in the whole of their Christian pilgrimage. Many are loth to tamper at all with the absolute commitment to such personal attainment in evangelism, for fear of weakening the challenge of discipleship, but it is perhaps here, more urgently than elsewhere, that the over-individualism of the revivalist legacy needs to be challenged. It is the corporate life and witness of the community of believers that bears the responsibility for this evangelistic task. As part of that witness, an individual may well attract many toward Christ throughout his or her life, but never specifically help a person take the step of faith – that particular moment may always seem to fall to someone else. That is not to lessen the call, it is not to rob anyone of the deep satisfaction of seeing another become a new person in Christ, for that is a joy to be owned by the whole fellowship, not just the 'trophy' of the gifted 'soul-winner'.

Missionary service overseas has been the supreme example of dedicated service for Christ within evangelicalism. This active and urgent spirituality is typified by C. T. Studd, the nineteenth-century socialite and cricketer turned missionary, who mused about how some 'like to live within the sound of church or

9 ibid., p. 188.

chapel bell' but how that he 'would rather run a rescue shop, within a yard of hell'.

Towards the close of the twentieth century, when understandings of overseas mission have undergone such major changes, this element has ceased to be as dominant as it was in former generations. Indeed, some of evangelicalism's uncertainties in the present may be due, in part, to its struggles in coming to terms with its spirituality of action when its main role-model, namely, the overseas missionary and the urgent call to serve God in foreign lands, has changed so radically. Though it may strike many as an exaggeration today, Torrey's challenge was the clarion call familiar within evangelicalism until the latter part of the twentieth century:

> God does not call everyone of us to go as foreign missionaries, but he does call many of us to go who are not responding to the call. Every Christian should offer himself for the foreign field and leave the responsibility of choosing him or refusing him to the all-wise One, God himself. No Christian has a right to stay at home until he has gone and offered himself definitely to God for the foreign field.[10]

The great majority of those who have responded to the call to leave home, friends, and country for the sake of the gospel have been women. It is fitting, therefore, to take the example of Amy Carmichael to illustrate this area of evangelical spirituality which focuses on identification with Christ as the servant of God – 'As the Father has sent me, so I send you' (John 20:21).

Amy Carmichael, from a Northern Irish Presbyterian background, went out with the Church of England Zenana Mission to India as the first missionary supported financially by the Keswick Convention. After an initial few months in Japan, she left England for India where she arrived on 9th November, 1895. She died there over fifty-five years later without ever returning home. In that half-century she founded the Dohnavur Fellowship, a work amongst needy children in South India, wrote nearly forty books (we looked at one of these, *If*, in chapter 4), most of which were best-sellers, and stands as a clear witness to the potency of the call to follow Christ wherever he may lead.

[10] R. A. Torrey, op. cit., p. 91.

Her life demonstrates the goal-orientation which controls so much of evangelical spirituality by its vocational and directional thrust.

Her widowed mother, when told of her twenty-five-year-old daughter's vocation to the mission field, was clear that the call of God was absolutely paramount; she wrote:

> Yes, dearest Amy, he has lent you to me all these years. He only knows what a strength, comfort and joy you have been to me. In sorrow he made you my staff and solace, in loneliness my more than child companion, and in gladness my bright and merry-hearted sympathizer. So, darling, when he asks you now to go away from within my reach, can I say nay? No, no, Amy, he is yours – you are his – to take you where he pleases and to use you as he pleases. I can trust you to him, and I do – and I thank him for letting you hear his voice as you have done.[11]

After her first months as a missionary in Japan, sickness forced Amy to return home – a move which fitted ill with her spirituality, as she wrote home in a letter; 'Talk of coming home! Did ever a soldier, worth calling one, run away at the first shot! Praise him – the pain is over now, and I am strong for the battle again.'[12] She has no problem in using what we would now consider too masculine a role model – the soldier in battle. For her it was a potent and appropriate image. The thought of retiring through ill-health struck her as desertion. This sense of obedience and duty was central to her Victorian brand of evangelical spirituality – indeed, it was one of evangelicalism's major contributions to Victorian culture in general. Such a concern with obedience and duty has survived somewhat better in evangelicalism than in society as a whole, but it may well be that, when future historians can see with clearer perspective, they will conclude that the weakening of the concepts of duty and obedience is one of the main ways in which late twentieth-century evangelicalism has been most affected by the spirit of the age. In which case, what evangelicalism gave to one age, it

[11] Frank Houghton, *Amy Carmichael of Dohnavur* (London, SPCK 1959), p. 46.
[12] ibid., p. 78.

manifestly failed to retain, when that age gave way to one which was very different in outlook.

Like her evangelical forebears, Amy Carmichael had a unitive view of mission; she made no separation between evangelism and caring for people's emotional, physical and social needs. The 'Memorandum of Association' of the Dohnavur Fellowship, which was founded as an independent mission in 1926, included this paragraph as an aim:

> To save children in moral danger; to train them to serve others; to succour the desolate and the suffering; to do anything that may be shown to be the will of our heavenly Father, in order to make his love known, especially to the people of India.[13]

The particular nature of the Fellowship's spirituality was also enshrined in the 'Memorandum of Association'. It reveals the strongly evangelical note of the ever-present God, personally involved in every decision and action of day-to-day living – a personal, even intimate view of providence. It lies behind the practice, more common in evangelicalism than within other traditions, of always surrounding every meal, meeting or gathering with prayer – prayer that consciously seeks to realize God's presence and looks for his guidance in any decisions that are made.

> The Leader with the help of the Council shall direct the conduct of the Fellowship according to the plans that God shall reveal. It is agreed that *the supreme Authority is vested in the unseen Leader, the Lord Jesus Christ*, while the human Leader seeks, in co-operation with the other members, to carry out the mind and will of the Divine.[14]

From a letter written home in 1896 we see Amy Carmichael's concern to keep a balance between the urgent activity of missionary service and the ability to trust God, to wait upon him, acknowledging his place as the director and energizer of mission: 'Do please, dear friends, ask that we may exchange the eagerness of the flesh for the earnestness of the Spirit and so

[13] ibid., p. 255.
[14] ibid., pp. 255f.

move in the force of that Holy Wind that we shall be carried
along by his great calm.'[15] We see here the concern of someone
deeply influenced by the Keswick movement – echoes of 'Let
go and let God'. But the activism, the urgency of the missionary
call was always present to keep this from sinking into a passive
quietism. Two years later she was writing home of the need for
fellow-workers who should be able to demonstrate an absolute
commitment to energetic evangelistic activity.

> O to be delivered from half-hearted missionaries! Don't
> come if you mean to turn aside for anything – for the
> 'claims of society' in the treaty ports and stations. Don't
> come if you haven't made up your mind to live for *one thing*
> – the winning of souls.[16]

But only some were called – it was only the few who went
abroad. It was inevitable that these missionaries should be seen
as the heroes of the faith. Consequently, back at home, much
of the spirituality centred more on supporting these heroes and
rejoicing with them in their success than in imitating them. A
certain service-by-proxy mentality was evident in this spirituality
of missionary support – as well as the triumphalism of those
who basked in the glory of the front-line troops – encouraged
also, no doubt, by the everyday thoughts of British imperialism.
Missionary hymns, such as this, by Priscilla Owens
(1829–1907), expressed the hope and confidence with which
the home supporter viewed the missionary endeavour.

> We have heard the joyful sound:
>   Jesus saves!
> Spread the gladness all around:
>   Jesus saves!
> Bear the news to every land,
> Climb the steeps and cross the waves;
> Onward – 'tis our Lord's command:
>   Jesus saves!

The final verse speaks of the sending church rejoicing in the

[15] Elisabeth Elliot, *Amy Carmichael* (Eastbourne, Marc 1988), pp. 126f.
[16] ibid., p. 142.

good news which, on every wind, wafts back to the faithful supporters:

> Give the winds a mighty voice:
>   Jesus saves!
> Let the nations now rejoice:
>   Jesus saves!
> Sing ye islands of the sea;
> Echo back, ye ocean caves;
> Shout salvation full and free:
>   Jesus saves!

But what if the winds did not bring back *cheerful* news? Occasionally there was the temptation to edit the news so that only a positive, triumphant story was heard, especially if extremely few quantifiable successes were all that resulted from the undoubted sacrifice and effort on the part of the missionaries. Many felt that tales for home consumption must be ones of progress and of triumph – another evidence, perhaps, of the triumphalism that can emerge out of the background of evangelical confidence in the gospel. But Amy Carmichael wanted to tell it as it was, and in her early years in India, the story of what she saw of other missionaries and managed to achieve herself was far from glamorous. At first her honest description of the realities and slowness of missionary work in India was turned down by the publishers as likely to upset and depress interest in overseas mission among its supporters in England – therefore leading to a loss in recruits and giving. After some intervention by others on her behalf, *Things As They Are* was published in 1903.

> It is more important that you should know about the reverses than about the successes of the war. We shall have all eternity to celebrate the victories, but we have only the few hours before sunset to win them. We are not winning them as we should, because the fact of the reverses is so little realized, and the needed reinforcements are not forthcoming, as they would be if the position were thoroughly understood . . . we have tried

to tell you the truth – the uninteresting, unromantic truth.[17]

Her honesty prevailed; the ungarnished truth was told. But it would be misleading to conclude from this instance that the home supporters of overseas mission were largely spectators who needed to hear exaggerated stories of missionary success in order to fuel their ongoing support. By and large they were enthusiastic and committed co-workers. Their support was given sacrificially – most obviously in terms of giving.

Giving to work overseas has long been in the forefront of evangelical charitable giving and, as such, is one of the duties within evangelical spirituality. Such giving is seen as clear evidence of committed discipleship. In writing of giving to overseas mission, Torrey strikes what many would accept as a central evangelical emphasis:

> Give systematically. Set aside for Christ a fixed portion of all the money or goods you get. Be exact and honest about it . . . The Christian is not under law, and there is no law binding on the Christian that he should give a tenth of his income, but as a matter of free choice and glad gratitude a tenth is a good proportion to begin with. Don't let it be less than a tenth.[18]

For many in the Church, tithing may seem a high standard to set, but while evangelicalism has often debated the difficulties of legalism which surround the practice of tithing, giving a tenth of one's income remains an acceptable guideline for many in their approach to giving as a spiritual duty.

Alongside giving, prayer is the other main activity in the spirituality of the home-supporter and co-worker in the overseas mission enterprise. Indeed, many have been eager to show a close spiritual link between these two duties of giving and prayer.

> Success and growth in the Christian life depend upon few things more than upon liberal giving. The stingy Christian cannot be a growing Christian. It is wonderful how a Christian man begins to grow when he begins to give.

[17] Amy Carmichael, *Things As They Are* (London, SPCK 1903), p. 158.
[18] R. A. Torrey, op. cit., pp. 94f.

> Power in prayer depends on liberality in giving . . . God's
> answers to our prayers come in through the same door that
> our gifts go out to others, and some of us open the door
> such a little way by our small giving that God is not able
> to pass into us any large answers to our prayers.[19]

Such teaching, if misunderstood, can be wrongly developed into
the discreditable and materialistic spirituality of the 'prosperity
gospel', but in essence, it emphasizes the holistic nature of the
life of faith. Earnestness in prayer and generosity in giving
equally and necessarily grow from the same root; they are each
encouraged by the other, and slackness in either discourages
the other. Spiritual effectiveness and sacrificial giving belong
inseparably together within evangelical spirituality. But whatever
the importance accorded to giving, the greatest work of the
missionary supporter has always been prayer and, in particular,
intercessory prayer which, because of its significance, must stand
on its own as the second major feature in the energetic activity
centre within evangelical spirituality.

Intercession, for God to Act

To be a missionary may be the most obvious way of joining in
God's activity, but prayer is involvement to the same degree.
To be involved through prayer for God's work in any place is
as vital as being involved in it by one's physical presence and
activity. Samuel Chadwick, one of the leading evangelical
Methodists in the earlier part of the twentieth century, declared
that 'the biggest thing in God's universe is a man who prays.
There is only one thing more amazing, and that is, that man,
knowing this, should not pray.'[20] To pray is not merely work, it
is *hard* work. It calls for fervour and commitment; it is an
energetic ministry as surely as is any more obviously front-line
physical presence within God's service. 'There is travail in it.
There is work in it. There is entreaty in it. There is importunity
in it. Maybe Coleridge was not far wrong when he spoke of
prayer as the highest energy of which the human heart is capable

[19] ibid., pp. 93f.
[20] Samuel Chadwick, *The Path of Prayer* (London, Hodder and Stoughton
1931), p. 8.

and the greatest achievement of the Christian's warfare on earth.'[21]

In evangelicalism, so committed to seeing God in action, intercession is at the very heart of prayer. It is this intercessory prayer which is the hardest work of all prayer. It demands daily consistency and, maybe, persistence over years, or even decades. It is work not only because of the energy it demands of us, but also because it is sharing in the very work of God.

> The normal function of prayer is to make intercession with God for others. That we may pray for others is the deepest mystery and the crowning glory of prayer . . . Nothing costs so much. St Paul speaks of being in travail, striving and labouring in prayer. There is always the sweat of blood in prevailing intercession . . . The prayer of intercession calls for intelligence, understanding, watchfulness, as well as for sympathy, intensity and sacrifice. There is often a severe discipline of patience and faith. Sometimes the answer comes immediately, and sometimes it tarries. The one truth in which faith rests is that it comes.[22]

There has rarely been much philosophical speculation about intercession within evangelicalism; its theology is succinctly stated as a mystery akin to some of the other deepest and most inscrutable truths of the faith. It is a way of being involved with Christ who himself is the great intercessor – once for all on the cross and now by his glorified presence at the right hand of the Father. 'In intercession,' wrote Andrew Murray, 'our King upon the throne finds his highest glory; in it we shall find our highest glory too. Through it he continues his saving work, and can do nothing without it; through it alone we can do our work, and nothing avails without it.'[23]

As with any work, it has to be approached with due care and thoughtfulness. The prayer list, and at times the careful logging of and thanksgiving for recognized answers to prayer, has been a feature of this commitment to intercession. It is the focus within evangelical spirituality which has always turned attention

[21] ibid., p. 47.
[22] ibid., pp. 69–73.
[23] Andrew Murray, *The Ministry of Intercession* (London, Nisbet 1897), p. 5.

outwards, away from the cultivation of one's own soul to a world-transforming orientation. Personal spiritual growth may well be a by-product of this central evangelical prayer activity, but cultivation of one's own relationship with God is not the purpose of prayer as it is in some other traditions. Prayer is, first and foremost, involvement in the mission of God within the world. Consequently, it is one of the most important tasks of the Church's leadership to encourage a commitment to intercession within the congregation.

> *God seeks intercessors.* – He sends his servants out to call them. Let ministers make this a part of their duty. Let them make their church a training school of intercession. Give the people definite objects for prayer. Encourage them to take a definite time to it, if it were only ten minutes every day.[24]

With such hard work envisaged there is great gain in mutual support and encouragement. There is also the promise of Jesus that he is present whenever two or three are gathered together in his name and will act if believers pray together in accordance with his will (Matthew 18:19, 20). These factors have led evangelicals to place a great importance on the prayer meeting, which has been a far more significant and consistent feature within corporate evangelical spirituality than has the practice of group Bible study (see chapter 6).

'It is not enough,' according to R. A. Torrey, 'that we have our times of secret prayer to God alone with him, we also need fellowship with others in prayer . . . The prayer-meeting is the most important meeting in the church. If your church has no prayer-meeting, use your influence to have one.'[25] The presence or absence of a prayer meeting has been seen as one of the main indicators of spiritual vitality within the local church. In speaking to fellow pastors, Charles Spurgeon held that the sad state of the Church was due to two factors – the grievous absence of any joint prayer meeting in many churches, and the formality and low level of attendance in many of those churches that do have such meetings. 'Oh, my brothers,' he pleaded, 'let

---

[24] ibid., p. 178.
[25] R. A. Torrey, op. cit., p. 80.

it be not so with you! Do train the people to continually meet together for prayer. Rouse them to incessant supplication. There is a holy art in it ... Believe me, if a church does not pray, it is dead. Instead of putting united prayer last, put it first. Everything will hinge upon the power of prayer in the church.'[26]

Half a century earlier in Scotland, Robert Murray McCheyne had been equally concerned about the powerless state of churches without prayer meetings. He was also aware of the importance of ensuring that, when they were a regular feature of the church's life, they should be meetings with God and not parades of piety and prowess in intercessory eloquence. In response to a request (in 1840) about prayer meetings, he included this advice in his reply:

> Meet weekly, at a convenient hour. Be regular in attendance. Let nothing keep you away from your meeting. Pray in secret before going. Let your prayers in the meeting be formed as much as possible on what you have read in the Bible. You will thus learn variety of petition, and a Scripture style. Pray that you may pray to God, and not for the ears of man. Feel his presence more than man's. Pray for the outpouring of the Spirit on the Church of Christ and for the world; for the purity and unity of God's children; for the raising up of godly ministers, and the blessing of those who are so already. Pray for the conversion of your friends, of your neighbours, of the whole town. Pray for the sending of the gospel to the Jews, and to the Gentile nations.[27]

Prayer meetings have emphasized the central evangelical truth that all believers are of equal importance and value as servants as well as children of God. This is the priesthood of all believers at its most inclusive and most visible. Prayer is the most vital work of all, and in their freedom of access to God, all can be at the very centre of his activity. No special training or commissioning is needed for this ministry; it is love, faith, hope

---

[26] Charles Spurgeon, *The Greatest Fight in the World* (1891, republished by Grace Publications 1972), p. 54. The book is the transcript of addresses given by Spurgeon at the last Pastors' Conference which he addressed.

[27] Andrew Bonar, *Memoir and Remains of Robert Murray McCheyne*, pp. 276f.

and passion that equip a person to minister in the prayer meeting. The weekly meeting for prayer has been one of the power houses within evangelical spirituality; it has been the central place of work; it remains the strongest testimony to the evangelical understanding of the place of intercessory prayer within the work of God in the world.

Power for Action

Exhaustion, listlessness, ineffectiveness, lack of success, powerlessness – these are some of the enemies of a spirituality with such an active thrust. The testimony throughout is consistent – it is the power of God's Spirit which is the vital resource needed for all the work of service and prayer.

The question to which countless thousands have returned in every generation of evangelical believers is: 'Why do I not have this power?' We are back again to the seemingly inescapable question of evangelical spirituality: 'Is there more?' Evangelical theology has usually been hesitant, if not hostile, in allowing a theological definition for any experience of God subsequent to conversion, but the spirituality of evangelicalism is constantly posing these questions of its theology. In chapter 5 we noticed this interrogation of theology by spirituality in relation to the quest for holiness; here we see it in relation to the need for spiritual power to accomplish what God requires, or, as many would rather express it, the power to achieve what God promises as possible for those who serve him faithfully. To illustrate this longing for power to serve God effectively, and the questions this has posed within evangelicalism, we look briefly at the experiences of two men, one American and one English, together with the theological evaluation of a Welshman.

The year 1871 was a critical one in the life of the evangelist D. L. Moody. He felt spiritually ill-equipped for the task which God had given him. Though he had seen many people converted he knew that he needed more from God. This is how his son describes this process:

> An intense hunger and thirst for spiritual power were aroused in him by two women who used to attend the meetings and sit on the front seat. He could see by the

expression on their faces that they were praying. At the close of the services they would say to him, 'We have been praying for you.' 'Why don't you pray for the people?' Mr Moody would ask. 'Because you need the power of the Spirit,' they would say.

'I need the power! Why,' said he in relating the incident years after, 'I thought I had power. I had the largest congregations in Chicago, and there were many conversions. I was in a sense satisfied. But right along those two godly women kept praying for me, and their earnest talk about anointing for special service set me thinking. I asked them to come and talk with me, and they poured out their hearts in prayer that I might receive the filling of the Holy Spirit. There came a hunger into my soul. I did not know what it was. I began to cry out as I never did before. I really felt that I did not want to live if I could not have this power for service.[28]

Very soon he had an experience of God's Spirit about which, ever afterwards, he was slow to speak because, in his words, it was 'almost too sacred an experience to name'. A close friend from Chicago, D. W. Whittle recorded his own account of Moody's experience: 'God blessed him with the *conscious* incoming to his soul of a presence and power of his Spirit such as he had never known before. His heart was broken by it. He spent much time in just weeping before God so overpowering was the sense of his goodness and love.'[29]

Evangelical theology in general has not easily coped with the questions posed by this kind of spiritual experience. One of those who brought such experience and theology together in a robust fashion was the Welshman, Martyn Lloyd-Jones. As one of the twentieth century's great evangelical preachers from the Reformed Puritan tradition, he often expressed severe criticism of many features of revivalist evangelism – yet he had no hesitation in putting Moody's experience of the power of God's

[28] W. R. Moody, *The Life of Dwight L. Moody* (Originally published in New York, 1900. London, Morgan and Scott. n.d.), pp. 132f.

[29] Whittle's diary for 2nd October, 1876, recorded in J. F. Findlay, *Dwight L. Moody* (Chicago University Press 1969), p. 132.

Spirit into a clear theological framework: 'That is the baptism of the Spirit,' he concluded. 'That is what turned D. L. Moody from a good, regular, ordinary minister, into the evangelist who was so signally used of God in this and in other countries.'[30]

Behind this judgement lay Lloyd-Jones' belief that 'it is possible to be a Christian without being baptized with the Spirit', an event which he described as 'something experimental, which is clear and unmistakable both to us and to those around us.'[31] In holding this view he stood out from many of his contemporary evangelicals, except, of course, some of those influenced by charismatic renewal. For his part, he held that he was describing 'the old evangelical view'[32] which he understood as making a distinction between saving faith received through regeneration by the Spirit, and power for service which is received through baptism with the Spirit. As he saw it, the Church stood in dire need of this empowering of the Spirit: 'There is this paramount need of authority, of power, of a holy boldness, of apostolic witness, if you like. It is the greatest need of all. And nothing can give us this but the baptism with the Spirit.'[33] However, evangelicals have traditionally been unhappy to subscribe to this or any other theological framework to explain spiritual crises subsequent to conversion.

For our second example we take Samuel Chadwick, born in Lancashire in 1860. He was no stranger to the second blessing holiness tradition of his Methodist background, but he did not believe that holiness could be achieved by such a route. He did, however, experience the gift of God's Spirit in a crisis experience.

> Early in the year 1882 there came to me an experience that lifted my life to a new plane of understanding and of power. I received the gift of the Holy Spirit ... I had neither power nor might in either service or prayer. I began to pray for power for service, and God led me to the answer by way of equipment for prayer. It was a great surprise to

[30] Martyn Lloyd-Jones, *Joy Unspeakable* (Eastbourne, Kingsway 1984), p. 80.
[31] ibid., p. 65.
[32] ibid., p. 270.
[33] ibid., p. 200.

me, for I thought I knew how to pray, and had prayed much over the work to which he had sent me.[34]

Together with a group of eleven others Samuel Chadwick had been praying for the empowering of the Spirit. He describes the result as an experience of Pentecost; it became the key to his future life and ministry. 'It gave me,' he said, 'a new joy and a new power, a new love and a new compassion. It gave me a new Bible and a new message. Above all else, it gave me a new understanding and a new intimacy in the communion and ministry of prayer; it taught me to pray in the Spirit.'[35]

Chadwick's experience of the power of the Spirit speaks in terms of both main areas in the evangelical call to work – active service and prayer. Indeed, as he explored further the relationship between the Spirit, power, and prayer he began to journey beyond the normal evangelical understandings of intercessory prayer and discovered a more contemplative framework for the work of prayer:

> Prayer is more than words, for it is mightiest when wordless. It is more than asking, for it reaches its highest glory when it adores and asks nothing . . . There are stages of prayer. In one stage we pray and ask him to help. There is a more wonderful way in which he prays and we assent, and his praying is ours . . . He it is that unifies hearts in prayer and makes them an irresistible unity in intercession.[36]

Presumably there will always be debates within evangelicalism about second (or multiple) infillings of the Holy Spirit, questions about a living experience of God, the way to holiness, and power for both service and prayer. But perhaps Chadwick's personal experience and his own reflection on that experience point us to the need to look at evangelical spirituality not just in its own terms, within its own particular theological framework, but from the perspective of other theological traditions. Chadwick moved through the intense energetic activity of evangelical intercessory prayer into a contemplative stillness which was also intercessory.

[34] Samuel Chadwick, op. cit., p. 36.
[35] ibid., p. 37.
[36] ibid., p. 40.

Perhaps the contemplative and mystical traditions of Christian spirituality hold many of the clues necessary in order to understand and explain evangelical spiritual experience.

Given the greater mutual openness which we are now beginning to experience between different Christian traditions, perhaps we can use our particular insights to help clarify further what is accepted within other spiritual traditions rather than using our own ammunition to demolish the other's experience.

8

A LIVING TRADITION

Not a burden we bear,
Not a sorrow we share,
But our toil he doth richly repay.

As the evangelical spiritual tradition approaches the latter part of its third century, it would be tempting to suggest an agenda for future direction. That would be a foolhardy undertaking. It would either be too personal to be of relevance to anyone else, or too arrogant an enterprise to be worth anybody's consideration.

As a more modest reflection on the tradition surveyed in the foregoing pages I suggest two tasks as one looks to the future of evangelical spirituality, in the hope that this will encourage others to work on their own more specific agendas – always conscious that the changes that have had such a major impact within the evolution of the tradition have resulted from the evolving faith of Christians as they have sought both to live true to the understandings of their age and culture, and also to challenge that culture where it has come into conflict with the gospel.

These tasks are chosen in the light of the present situation in many evangelical circles – the growing openness to other traditions. Evangelicalism has, of necessity if for no other reason, to face the opportunities and problems in this substantially new situation. The first task is to explore what is involved in maintaining and promoting vitality within the living and evolving tradition of evangelical spirituality. The second is to re-examine specific emphases within one's own tradition, which we all need to do afresh in each generation, both individually and communally. For this second task I take, as an example, one model, intercession, that has a solid evangelical pedigree, in the hope of bringing some focus to the direction in which evangelical spirituality could profitably move as it approaches the beginning of its fourth century.

MAINTAINING THE VITALITY OF A TRADITION

Identification with the historical tradition of the community of faith is the first requirement for its ongoing vitality in the present. For the continuing life of any organism – spirituality included – there must be a healthy relationship between the roots and today's fresh growth. It is on the basis of our understanding of the tradition in which we have been nurtured that we can develop our own authentic faith for today. But with the diminishing awareness of historical rootedness which is one of the features of contemporary culture, evangelicals, as so many others, are much less aware of their tradition than in former generations. Because, at the same time, we are becoming open to other traditions and ready to be questioned by them, we are confronted with considerable problems. Unless we have an understanding of the history of our own tradition we are not able to enter into any meaningful encounter and dialogue with other emphases, in a way that can lead to an integrated and growing spiritual life.

One of the main problems with this situation is that individuals may well jettison parts of their spiritual tradition which do not seem to suit them in the immediate present, and take on board ideas and practices that seem to fit their situation a little better, without necessarily understanding what they are doing to the integrity either of their own spirituality or that from which they are borrowing. The danger is clear – Christians can end up with a jumbled mixture of spiritual delicacies which fail to relate to each other except on any other basis than the existential needs which they had at different points in their journey. When it subsequently dawns upon them, as it inevitably will, that their situation and their felt needs are very different, then the 'pick n' mix' spiritual diet which they have evolved will not fit; it will appear in its true light – a disparate set of spiritual practices and beliefs. This will feel like chaos and, in all probability, lead to a total abandonment of faith.

At its most gloomy this is the prospect for life and faith without history and tradition. It goes a long way to explain why some Christians, seemingly some of the keenest disciples on earth, with all the latest commitments and visions of intense faith can, the very next week, be totally lost. The step from super-spiritual commitment (where the real basis is a non-integrated set of enthusiasms) to non-believing chaos is a very short step indeed. It is one of the reasons why pastors, priests, and spiritual guides become more cautious about new spiritual enthusiasms as they grow in wisdom and experience within pastoral ministry and spiritual direction. Their awareness of the potential for spiritual chaos is an ever-present challenge to their desire to encourage deeper adventures into faith, prayer, and the vision of God.

Most evangelicals recognize the role of the ordained ministry as being the guardians and teachers of the tradition, and seldom has the need for teaching the tradition been more important than it is today. In part there has been a failure to equip people to face the new openness and pluralism of our age from the sure confidence of 'knowing who we are and where we have come from'. But this is not a plea for a return to the 'good old days', re-entering the fort, or even returning to the former securities. Some words of Max Warren about our relationship to history provide helpful insight into the necessary integration in spirituality between our own personal experience and journey, and the spiritual tradition in which we are being nurtured. It is an approach that serves well as a basic framework for us all, whatever our tradition, as we seek to receive from what God has been doing in our corporate history, and move forward with him in an authentic living encounter today.

> I believe that history matters tremendously and that we must take the past as seriously as we hope the future will take us . . . I do not idolise the past. I am not a conservative in the common meaning of that term. I am deeply convinced that we sometimes keep faith with the past best by making some new departure which will, in fact, fulfil what in the past was being attempted in other ways. But I make this departure in fellowship-with-the-past and not in any sort of contemptuous antagonism for it. As it were, I try

and enter into conversation with the past, make it my contemporary, argue with it and treat it as a living companion. I do not believe we can understand the present and plan for the future unless we see clearly how continuous the present is with the past and how all-pervading is the influence of past patterns upon present behaviour.[1]

Cross-fertilization within the Christian Spiritual Tradition

Given an attitude to one's own spiritual tradition which is thankful but critical, iconoclastic yet affirming, we can begin to benefit from the greater openness to other traditions which is such a feature of the pluralism of our age. It is something to be welcomed as a gift and opportunity from God, rather than to be feared and rejected as an unwelcome feature of our culture. Complementarity between different Christian spiritualities holds out the prospect of greater treasures to explore, deepening insight into one's own tradition, and broader and more detailed possibilities along the walk of faith. Evangelicals, like others, are called to enter into a symbiotic relationship with other spiritual traditions. This process recognizes the value and distinctiveness of our own position and heritage, but understands and welcomes the mutual benefits that result from the organic relationships between different parts of the body.

When evangelicalism lets down the barricades and begins to explore the diverse traditions within the Church it can discover wealth where once it saw only dross, though anything it sees will be mixed, as it knows so well from its own history. Consequently, discernment is central in spiritual exploration. But it is of the essence of evangelicalism to encourage each individual believer to launch out on the adventure of faith, standing in the grace of God, testing all by the scriptures, and dependent on the Spirit's direction and discernment. In this process we are seeking to strengthen and broaden our own spirituality to provide a faithful, relevant and coherent basis for the whole of life.

[1] Quoted in F. W. Dillistone, *Into All The World* (London, Hodder and Stoughton 1980), p. 80.

The Renewing of the Renewal

As the foregoing pages have shown, charismatic renewal has been a major innovation within the general development of evangelical spirituality in the second half of the twentieth century. It looks as though the impact on evangelical belief and practice has been so pervasive that its influence in the twenty-first century will match the impact made on twentieth-century evangelicalism by the Keswick movement and revivalism, both of which arose in the latter part of the nineteenth century. Just as those two movements were, in part, a product of Romanticism and Victorian aspirations, so charismatic renewal is, in part, a manifestation of Modernism's search for authentic individual experience, and Democracy's influence on the nature of the Church as an open institution. This in no way denies the possibility of seeing charismatic renewal as part of what God is saying to his people.

As a movement, it still poses many unanswered questions to evangelical theology and spirituality. By way of example, one of the sharpest is concerned with the manner, extent and limits of God's revelation. One of the strongest features which seems to gain in theological importance within most forms of evangelical-charismatic spirituality is the issue of prophecy – how far is God's revelation confined to the pages of scripture? Some forms of evangelicalism have found themselves wanting to say, 'In every way!' This is the kind of answer intended to eliminate all possibility of God speaking through a contemporary prophetic word today and thus seeming to re-open questions about revelation which evangelicalism had hoped were satisfied by the answers given in yesterday's debates. But, as a tactic, it will not do; it is untrue to some of the roots within the tradition itself. There has always been the conviction that God does speak directly to individuals – he is a God who intervenes within the particular circumstances of our daily lives; this is an evangelical distinctive. Charismatic renewal poses the question: 'Can prophecy occupy a place within this theological context?' Clearly there are broader questions to be faced at a communal level in relation to scripture, discernment and the life of the local church – these are issues with which evangelicalism may well find itself grappling for many years to come until its accumulated wisdom is able to discover the right ways of modifying or accommodating those features in this area which prove to be genuine.

There is evidence, as we have already noted, that charismatic renewal has sometimes been the bridge toward greater integration between differing spiritualities. For instance, the contemplative and mystical tradition of the Church becomes more accessible through some charismatic approaches to prayer, as was recognized by the Church of England Doctrine Commission. In their examination of this area of spirituality they observed that charismatics and contemplatives converge 'in that profound, though often fleeting or obscure, sense of entering in prayer into a 'conversation' *already in play*, a reciprocal divine conversation between Father and Spirit which can finally be reduced neither to divine monologue nor to human self-transcendence.'[2] For many evangelicals, contemplation, picture, symbol, sacrament, colour, dance, drama, and the like, have become part of the widened horizons of their spirituality through the influence, personal or communal, of charismatic renewal. These are part of the evidence of the vitality of evangelicalism as a living and evolving tradition.

Diverse Roots of Integrative Growth within the Tradition

There are clues to life-promoting integration between evangelicalism and the wider tradition of the Church that emerged long before the advent of charismatic renewal. In Wesley, as we have observed, there were emphases fostered by Catholic spirituality as well as by his Protestant heritage. In Spurgeon one sees a kind of Jesus-mysticism, especially in his sermons on the Song of Solomon, which match many of the expressions of love, devotion and intimacy towards Jesus which one can find, for instance, in Julian of Norwich. Frances Ridley Havergal's account of her intense spiritual experience which she called 'consecration' reveals clear evidence of the mystical tradition. Exploring her experience a little further we notice an intensity, a givenness, even a passivity about the situation – 'He himself,' she records, 'showed me all this clearly.'[3] Her particular experi-

---

[2] *We Believe in the Holy Spirit*, p. 36.
[3] M. V. G. Havergal (ed.), *Memorials of Frances Ridley Havergal* (James Nisbet and Co. 1980), p. 126.

ence of the sovereign grace of God, as with many in the mystical tradition, endured as a basic insight in her understanding of God and his purposes for her. There is the typical mystical combination of the intense longing for God and the gracious giving of God in his meeting with the believer in the individuality of her own spiritual journey. 'He himself had shown her that there were "regions beyond" of blessed experience and service,' explains Frances' sister in her comments on this experience; 'he had kindled in her very soul the intense desire to go forward and possess them; and now, in his own grace and love, he took her by the hand and led her into the goodly land.' She went on to describe Frances' experience in words which reflect both the universal mystical traditions of the Church and the Romanticism of her age. God 'lifted her whole life into sunshine, of which all she had previously experienced was but as pale and passing April gleams compared with the fulness of summer glory.'[4]

As we have seen, in relation to the search both for holiness and for spiritual power, evangelicalism has often struggled with viewing this as a second blessing; the option has usually been either to include it somewhere within a doctrinal framework of the various parts of the life of faith in its linear progression, or to describe it as a blind alley. The mystical tradition, while seeming to leave more loose ends from the linear perspective of the evangelical, offers a fuller context in which to evaluate this kind of experience of God's grace. The linear, democratic and egalitarian strand, so marked within evangelicalism, has, at times, left little place for God to work in markedly different ways in the spiritual experience of different individuals, solely upon the basis of his free choice. This hesitancy may well stem from the right concern that salvation is equally and freely available to all, with no place for merit, and no special class of holy people. But, within this spiritual egalitarianism, one needs space for the unpredictable within the operation of God in the intimacy of the individual's relationship with him, which usually cannot easily be fitted into a universally valid linear understanding of the work of God's grace from justification to glorification. In stressing an egalitarianism of status, evangelical spirituality sometimes insists on an egalitarianism of encounter, fearing that

---

[4] ibid., pp. 125–6.

the former is compromised if the latter is abandoned. Other traditions of the Church may well not have emphasized as clearly the freedom and equality of all in relation to salvation, but they have often borne witness to the sovereign freedom of God in the individuality of his encounter with each in their spiritual journey. The experiences of spiritual direction, from the fourth-century Desert Fathers onwards, has accumulated a wealth of insight into the workings of God within the individual which both contains pointers to diverse ways of spiritual exploration and also offers clues for the understanding and evaluation of individual experience within the broad parameters of the evangelical and biblical understanding of the life of faith.

Two Reforming Traditions within Spirituality

To illustrate this integrative encounter with other spiritual traditions, evangelicalism may well find itself taking a journey of exploration from its homelands in northern Europe (where the sixteenth-century Protestant Reformation was born) to southern Europe, to the home of two Spaniards, Teresa of Avila and Ignatius Loyola. These were near-contemporaries of each other and were the great reforming figures within sixteenth-century Spain. They have rarely been seen in this light by Protestants, who have traditionally only known them through their roles within the Counter-Reformation and the Inquisition. But each of these figures can provide clues for evangelical spirituality as it enters into a fuller dialogue with its own history – it may well be able to integrate features that were by-passed in former ages but which have now become accessible to the children of the spiritual renewal which has its roots in northern Europe.

Teresa of Avila provides the highly developed image of the *Interior Castle*[5] as a model to help us understand the encounter between God and the individual. For those basing their approach to spirituality on the evangelical understanding of the process of sanctification, leading from justification to glorification, Teresa provides insight into *how* the individual moves

[5] A helpful English text is *The Interior Castle* edited by Halcyon Backhouse (London, Hodder and Stoughton 1988). A stimulating introduction to Teresa's life and spirituality can be found in Rowan Williams, *Teresa of Avila* (London, Geoffrey Chapman 1991).

forward, and around, and deeper, and upwards, within the spiritual journey. There is a fluidity about her Castle – it is like a crystal: in some senses, one passes in a linear way from the first mansion on towards the seventh, but then different parts are visible at the same time within our journey, and it cannot be mapped out in a logical way even for a particular individual. There are different progressions for different individuals, with the gifts of God coming in different form and intensity to different people at different times within the shape of their own particular journey. Teresa's own life of prayer, and the wisdom she gained through guiding others, gives her insight into obedience, humility, self-knowledge, spiritual warfare, emotion, practical service, visions, contemplation, disorientation, darkness and union with God, all communicated within the cautious enthusiasm that colours her encouragement to each of us in pursuing our own encounter with God. Her practical wisdom, her concern to help others to progress in prayer, and her own discoveries about the life of prayer, make her an accessible guide to many evangelicals who will see in her a kindred spirit, though divided by so many cultural and historical divisions, as well as doctrinal differences. For many, it is her own openness that first wins them over:

> My readers must have patience with me just as I have with myself as I write about subjects that I don't understand. But really, sometimes, I take up the paper, like a complete idiot with no idea what to say or how to begin . . . for though we are always being told what a good thing prayer is, and our constitutions require us to spend many hours a day in prayer, we are only told what we have to do; we are given very little instruction about the supernatural work of the Lord within the soul.

Many find that their own tradition gives them a similar sense of duty about prayer but very little help in understanding the dynamics and practicalities of this privilege and ministry.

Teresa was from a Jewish family, forcibly converted under the edict of the Catholic monarchs of Spain. She is a focus of reform within the Western spiritual tradition, but at the same time, marked out as one who had recently emerged from a very different religious tradition. She often found little acceptance from many within the Catholic Church of her day, and not infrequently encountered hostility. She occupies a symbolic position within the history and development of spirituality – a symbol of the outsider who is yet a renewing presence within the major spiritual tradition. With a degree of historical irony, she provides an intriguing symbol for the ongoing development within evangelical spirituality.

For other evangelicals, encouragement may come more immediately from Teresa's fellow-countryman. Many have already been introduced to *The Spiritual Exercises* of Ignatius, and to his particular way of scriptural meditation and prayer, by the modern-day Jesuit Gerard Hughes, in what has become a 'modern classic' – *God of Surprises*.[6] At the heart of *The Spiritual Exercises* lies a thoroughly evangelical concern – the journey of renewed obedience based on conversion, and following the will of God for each individual as he reveals this through meditation on the scriptures. Thirty-day (and now, seven-day) retreats are the normal ways of working through the *Exercises* with the guidance of a spiritual director, and while these are seldom part of the experience of many evangelicals, the disciplined approach to growth and vocational direction through imaginative meditation on the scriptures, and listening to the inner voice of God as he speaks through his Word, has grafted well into a thoroughly faithful evangelical understanding of the life of faith.

These two examples, of Teresan prayer and Ignatian spirituality, are but instances of the richness within the universal Christian spiritual tradition which can provide sources of ongoing renewal for people within the historic evangelical tradition. This process is clearly part of the pluralism of our age, but it is just as valid to see it as an opportunity, given by God, to explore more of the extensive spiritual resources within the corporate experience of the Body of Christ as we face the demands of the wider pluralism of secular outlooks and other faith communities which are facing the Christian with a whole new set of questions and challenges today.

---

[6] Gerard Hughes, *God of Surprises* (London, Darton, Longman and Todd 1985). As with Teresa of Avila, Halcyon Backhouse has also edited a popular English version of Ignatius' work, *The Spiritual Exercises of Ignatius Loyola* (London, Hodder and Stoughton 1989).

A Tradition that Brings Wholeness and Life

There is a danger in this wider spiritual exploration; the danger that we will compound one of the traditional mistakes inherent in most spiritualities, rather than discovering authentic strength in God for life and witness in the pluralistic age in which we live. The issue that has most brought spiritual stagnation and ineffectiveness, when it envisaged the opposite, has been the compartmentalization of life falsely into the spiritual and the secular. This is especially a continuing danger for spirituality in our secularized Western cultures today which encourage us to live with a set of values common to society as a whole, yet developing an internal privatized spirituality which suits each of us as individuals. Evangelicalism has often faced the danger of encouraging super spiritualities that are not integrated within a full vision of personhood and humanity. In the exploration of other spiritual traditions it is easy (blindly, yet enthusiastically) to fall ever more deeply into that trap, now that the prevailing cultural attitudes encourage such privatization and compartmentalization.

Evangelicalism, in common with most of Western Christianity, has often displayed a dualism between affectivity and the intellect. Any development of the tradition must be wary of perpetuating such a dislocation of personhood. However, the danger with modern aspirants in their encounter with God may be less in that direction, but more in the sacred-secular, or self-cultivation versus world-orientated compartmentalization – and both of these have precedents within evangelicalism which can find plenty of allies in other traditions. The marrying of two such hybrid spiritualities produces a specimen far too weak for the demands of life and mission in today's world.

A SPIRITUALITY OF INTERCESSION

To illustrate this task of renewing and enhancing the tradition, I conclude with a brief look at one specific area – *Intercession*. More than any other spiritual tradition evangelicalism has earned the right to be called a spirituality of intercession. It is intercession, as we have seen, which holds the high ground in the evangelical approach to prayer. It is the type of prayer which follows in the footsteps of the great biblical intercessors like Moses, who is a powerful statement of the effectiveness of intercession as entering into partnership with God – 'The LORD was so angry with Aaron that he was ready to destroy him, but I interceded also on behalf of Aaron at that same time' (Deuteronomy 9:20).

Intercession Directs Prayer Outwards

The placing of intercession at the heart of prayer takes the centre of our concern away from our own psychological and emotional needs. It frees spirituality from the cult of narcissistic self-culture which is often apparent in recent developments in all types of spirituality. It turns attention to God's glory and the needs of others. It turns the focus from building a comfortable community within the Church, in which we can be peaceably and harmoniously protected, towards extending the boundaries of the kingdom of God into the world. It catapults us from the ultimately destructive effects of individual and communal strategies of inner-protectiveness into the expansive arena of the mission of God. The evangelical commitment to intercession ensures the centrality of *the God who acts* as a focus of spirituality alongside *the God who is* – the latter aspect of God is increasingly seen by many as the appropriate concern in spirituality, but if this becomes an exclusive focus it is one that is both dangerous for healthy spiritual life, and wrong!

The growth of the significance of groups which are concerned with mutual sharing and caring can again reflect this same inward tendency in spirituality. The traditional evangelical understanding of the corporate ministry of intercession within the prayer meeting is due for an eruptive re-birth. At a time when the growth of informality and a concern for spiritual renewal is leading many in all traditions to emphasize the importance of group activities, it is vital that this move learns from the evangelical commitment to group intercession, as well as developing structures for mutual support and encouragement.

In reflecting on Moses' ministry of intercession, the psalmist employs the analogy of 'standing in the breach'. In this common Old Testament image the intercessor is seen as the one who stands in the breach in the city walls when the defences have been broken down, because of attack, erosion, misfortune or carelessness. It is the place of weakness through which all kinds of danger can pass. 'Therefore he said he would destroy them – had not Moses, his chosen one, stood in the breach before him, to turn away his wrath from destroying them' (Psalm 106:23).

The prayer of intercession is the task in which the believer stands in the gap where others' vulnerability is most apparent. It is a defensive more than an aggressive posture. It is the prayer that doggedly persists as long as the other remains in danger. The prophecy of Ezekiel bears symbolic witness to the place and value of this ministry of intercession. Its absence leaves the vulnerable unprotected and exposed: 'And I sought for anyone among them who would repair the wall and stand in the breach before me on behalf of the land, so that I would not destroy it; but I found no one' (Ezekiel 22:30).

Intercession is standing in the place of spiritual vulnerability on behalf of those who cannot pray, or have forgotten how to – in the place of those who refuse to pray, or who need others to stand alongside them to support them in their own lonely struggles in prayer. Intercession is the parish priest leading in prayer at a funeral service when people are often painfully aware of the enormous gaping hole that has appeared in their lives, not only the loss of someone close to them, but also the vulnerability of realizing that all of life's security has been radically questioned and they feel frighteningly exposed. Intercession is also the prayer of the neighbour when a friend faces redundancy and experiences the gap opening wide – the sense of meaninglessness, perhaps, or the rejection of former colleagues who need to protect themselves from every reminder of what could happen. The individual intercessor, and the interceding prayer group will, above all, be concerned for those who are 'without hope and without God in the world', for whom the gap needing to be bridged is of eternal dimensions.

Intercession Moves Prayer on to the Streets

As intercession deepens our concern for God's glory and the need of others, so it has a spacial and re-locating effect in our spirituality. It drives prayer out of the sanctuary and into the street, whether the sanctuary be a service in the church building, a prayer meeting in a home, or a person's secret time of private prayer. Some of the recent developments in evangelical and charismatic circles have borne witness to this move on to the streets in events like the marches for Jesus and the songs which accompany this approach – intercession is being acted out in the arena where the kingdom of God confronts the forces of darkness, sin and unbelief.

This development is in line with the long tradition of open-air witness within evangelicalism. The concern is to take the gospel on to the secrets and not to entomb it within the sacred buildings where so few ordinary people ever go; buildings which are still seen by many as the preserve of the socially respectable. Evangelicals have often been prepared to stand the ridicule of their 'cultured despisers' because of the deep sense of calling to present Christ where the Church is manifestly failing in its task. At its best, this tough unselfconscious streak within evangelical spirituality is a necessary injection of steel into an often effete and ineffective Church. But there are questions that evangelicals need to ponder in 'marching for Jesus' as an effective means of taking witness and intercession on to the streets. There is the possibility of missing two vital ingredients as we translate intercession into the public arena. It can be a more aggressive triumphalistic approach than the defensive posture of the calling of the intercessor as the one who stands in the breach. Intercession is bridging the gap between the needy and God in order to be a channel for the victory of God, rather than moving out to take on the enemy in offensive combat. This may seem a quibble over a symbol, but it is far more than that. It is to do with how we understand ourselves to be co-workers with God, where we see the problem to be, and how the grace of God operates through human agency. The second concern is to do with the manner of intercession in public. To return to the biblical models, Mordecai 'was powerful among the Jews and popular with his many kindred, for he sought the good of his people and interceded for the welfare of all his descendants' (Esther 10:3). Here we see how intercession includes the move from prayer toward God into action in the human arena. Intercession includes both as part of the same activity. It is one of the strengths of a spirituality centred on intercession that there is no division between prayer and action: intercession is both. It is both the intercession group praying for the friend who is being hounded by the bailiffs in a repossession squabble, and also attending the court to stand up for them in the face of the authorities – and, if appropriate, helping to close up the financial gap that remains. Taking intercession on to the streets means taking action, at least as much as praying in public.

Intercession Leads to Contemplation

As Samuel Chadwick discovered (see chapter 7), intercession need not be wordy, it can be silent, wordless prayer. This is a part of intercession where evangelicals could often learn much from other traditions. To stand in the breach is to *be there* for others, not necessarily to be saying anything. The words are unimportant in comparison with the presence. It is the ministry of God's Spirit to provide the words to the one who is standing at the place of intercession. 'Likewise the Spirit helps us in our weakness; for we do not know how to pray as we ought, but that very Spirit intercedes with sighs too deep for words. And God, who searches the heart, knows what is the mind of the Spirit, because the Spirit intercedes for the saints according to the will of God' (Romans 8:26,27). The lack of knowledge of what to say, the inability to form words in prayer, is no hindrance to intercession. Indeed such silence and wordlessness may be one of the clearest signs that a person is in the place where intercession is a powerfully central part of the immediate purposes of God. As we grow in this ministry of intercession so its links with contemplative prayer become clearer. This is something recognized very clearly by Michael Ramsey (at times, himself, a critic of evangelical spirituality):

> *Intercede* does not mean to speak or to plead or to make requests or petitions: it means to meet someone, to be with someone in relation to or on behalf of others. Jesus is with the Father for us. And our prayer means essentially our being with God, putting ourselves in his presence, being hungry and thirsty for him, wanting him, letting heart and mind and will move towards him; with the needs of our

world on our heart. It is a rhythmic movement of our personality into the eternity and peace of God and no less into the turmoil of the world for whose sake as for ours we are seeking God. If that is the heart of prayer, then the contemplative part of it will be large. And a Church which starves itself and its members in the contemplative life deserves whatever spiritual leanness it may experience.[7]

Words, of course, remain important, especially in corporate prayer because they are the way of making the intercession a consciously corporate activity in which all can join with equal conviction. Often, the absence of words in a prayer meeting says that very little prayer is going on! But there are also those periods of intense silence within a prayer meeting which speak powerfully both of the sense of God's presence and the reality and effectiveness of intercession.

Intercession is the Activity of Heaven

Evangelical spirituality and worship has often lacked the dimension of heaven, and the communion of saints. The ministry of intercession takes our prayer and worship into the inner sanctum of heaven, to the central eternal role of the Son of God: 'Who is to condemn? It is Christ Jesus, who died, yes, who was raised, who is at the right hand of God, who indeed intercedes for us' (Romans 8:34; and also Hebrews 7:25).

In intercession we enter into the heavenly ministry of Christ. Worship brings us to that place – therefore, worship is part of intercession. Such an awareness gives a new dimension to how the evangelical Quiet Time has normally been understood in so far as there has not been a major emphasis on worship in this personal discipline. Charismatic renewal has brought some new input into this area – particularly in corporate times of intercession where worship and intercession are seen to be intricately intertwined activities. My own experience for three years in a community of reconciliation in Northern Ireland taught me more about this than had been present in my own evangelical understanding up to that point. In the two separate hours of

---

[7] Michael Ramsey, *Canterbury Pilgrim* (London, SPCK 1974), pp. 59–60.

prayer, which were the daily focus of our community life, the thrust was always intercession for peace and reconciliation in Church and nation, but the major activity was worship. It was that rhythmic movement, which Ramsey describes, of being with God in worship with the needs and situations of the people in our hearts: worship was very specifically intercession – standing in the gap that persists as a gaping sore in the island of Ireland. But the worship was not determined by words about 'the Troubles'; rather it centred on glorifying Christ, the heavenly Intercessor.

Intercession Points us to the Cross of Christ

It is at the cross that the great prayer and act of intercession took place: 'Therefore I will allot him a portion with the great, and he shall divide the spoil with the strong; because he poured out himself to death, and was numbered with the transgressors; yet he bore the sin of many, and made intercession for the transgressors' (Isaiah 53:12). In the last analysis, evangelicalism is a spirituality of intercession because it is a spirituality of the cross. Whatever the more immediate concerns of evangelicalism at any point in its history this is likely to remain the one thing that it presents continually to the rest of the Church as the centre of faith and spirituality.

It is the presence of this great act of intercession which has so often provided the gravitational pull back to soundness and orthodoxy when factions within evangelicalism have been enticed into some enthusiastic by-way or spiritual exoticism. Amidst the recurring tendencies to triumphalism, the cross preserves the integrity of the servant of God, interceding at the point of vulnerability between earth and heaven. One of Graham Kendrick's best-loved songs provides a strong restatement of the heart of evangelical spirituality.

> From heaven you came,
> Helpless babe,
> Entered our world,
> Your glory veiled;
> Not to be served
> But to serve,

And give your life
That we might live.
This is our God,
The Servant King,
He calls us now
To follow him,
To bring our lives
As a daily offering
Of worship to
The Servant King.

Any spirituality that focuses on intercession has a powerful bias towards recognizing the place of vulnerability within the activity of Christ on the cross, and within the spirituality of those who seek to follow him. In the words of another of Graham Kendrick's songs, it is a spirituality of 'Meekness and Majesty'. The Servant King interceded for us in the humiliation of the cross, and intercedes for us in the glory of heaven. Evangelical spirituality not only pleads with others to keep this centre stage, but ever stands itself under the judgement of the cross when it fails to embrace the pain within the victory, the humiliation within the power. The third verse of 'The Servant King' contains the central invitation of this spirituality of intercession:

Come, see his hands
And his feet,
The scars that speak
Of sacrifice,
Hands that flung stars
Into space
To cruel nails
Surrendered.
This is our God,
The Servant King...